SOUTHWEST MINNESOTA

Southwest
MINNESOTA

the Land

and the People

David R. Pichaske & Joseph Amato, editors

CROSSINGS PRESS 2000   MARSHALL, MINNESOTA

Interior design by Shari De Graw
Cover design by David Pichaske

Published by Crossings Press, Marshall, Minnesota.

ISBN 0-9614119-8-8

00   01   02   03   04   5   4   3   2   1

CONTENTS

ACKNOWLEDGMENTS

Our thanks are many and our gratitude is deep. It could not be otherwise in an anthology which required so many writers to write new pieces for us, and so many authors and publishers to give us permission to reprint previously published work.

Additionally this work requires a lengthy institutional acknowledgment. Southwest State University's English Department, its newly formed Rural and Regional Studies Center, and its History Center lent time and resources to this work. The Southwest State University administration provided release time and resources to this project so that it would materialize itself into a book and a conference that would stage an encounter between writers and historians over rendering the meaning of rural experience.

Again, as has become almost a ritual in acknowedging funding for rural and regional publications, we express our thanks to the Otto Bremer Foundation, the Minnesota Humanities Commission, the Society for the Study of Local and Regional History, and the University's own Gunlogson Fund. They continue to show that they believe that knowledge matters to the countryside.

PREFACE

"This region has more writers *per capita* than anywhere else in the country," people told me when I arrived in southwestern Minnesota two decades ago. "But we have not many *capitas*."

They weren't kidding. Southwestern Minnesota, Eastern South Dakota, Northwestern Iowa—the territory Frederick Manfred named "Siouxland"—can legitimately claim a disproportional share of the Midwest's (and the nation's) writers, despite a landscape that was underpopulated when I got here and shrinks as I write. The problem seems to be that writers, like everyone except farmers and implement salesmen, must escape this region to find themselves and make it in the big world. Still, most seem to carry with them the stamp of this hauntingly sparse landscape, and many return to homes once abandoned, to native villages once spurned . . . and to writers' festivals at Southwest State University.

Early in my life here I conceived the idea of gathering an anthology of Siouxland writers (stretched a bit to include Rolvaag and Keillor, but not, alas, to reach Tom McGrath): the old and the new, the visitors and their hosts, the ancient people, as Meridel Le Sueur called them, and the newly come. That project got sidetracked, as projects do,

while the ranks of writers kept expanding. Meanwhile, perhaps intimidated by the competition and feeling too much the newcomer to pretend deep ties with the territory, I turned gradually from words to photographs: material mostly in minor key, lone cottonwoods and abandoned machinery, evidence of a depopulation which escapes the attention of Twin Cities visitors. There was something honest in a photograph which made it seem less an artistic construct than the essay or story. Not that I caught my Southwest Minnesota writer friends in lies or enhancements; it just seemed to me that sometimes, in the words of one of my students, the writers seemed sometimes to live in a reality of the imagination.

Another thing I noticed is that people would flip casually through the pages of Bill Holm's *The Music of Failure* or my own *Poland in Transition* looking mainly at the photos and say, without having read a word of text, "nice book." I quit kidding myself: a picture is indeed worth a thousand words. Books need pictures.

So the anthology of Southwest Minnesota writers became a photo-text book, a coffee table kind of book, part of a genre I ceased to dismiss when Paul Gruchow and Gerald Brimacombe produced *Travels*

in Canoe Country, when Bill Holm and Bob Firth produced *A Landscape of Ghosts.* I kept reading books and photographing not so much a landscape but, as Willa Cather puts it, elements of which a landscape might be composed. Joe Amato and I imagined a photo-text album presenting the region through my images and the words of its best writers, although two are missing, with contextual essays by authorities on the region's geography and people. Because both processes continued independent of each other, the photos were not shot with particular texts in mind. Nor are photos always matched with texts on the level of illustration. Photos and text are intended to complement each other to produce a portrait of southwestern Minnesota's land and people. One day perhaps Joe, I, and the region's writers can offer a second volume focusing on Southwestern Minnesota's towns and farms . . . and a third volume on the area's institutions.

I'd like to thank Joe for his help in framing this idea and this book. And I especially want to thank Angela Arvidson, a remarkable woman wiser than her years, more colleague than student. Both Joe and Angela kept pushing me when I might have become distracted. Thanks to Sandy Mosch for help and criticism, and of course to the writers and their publishers for permission to reprint material here. I hope readers of this book will work their way upstream to the sources of these texts, then buy and read those books, and perhaps share those books with friends. Maybe even write a fan letter to authors still living. The landscape nourishes and sustains a writer, but part of that landscape is human, and sustenance comes in the form of audience response. Only bad writers write in a placeless vacuum, and you, good reader, must be part of the non-vacuum of Southwestern Minnesota.

—David Pichaske, June, 1999

FOREWORD

Writers of fiction and non-fiction define and value our lives. Their works delineate our natural, social, and moral landscapes by shaping the contour of our senses, the richness of our past, and the reach of our moral imagination. Without them we are mere fragments of what we could be.

Because we are so indebted to writers, we must suspect them. The most trusted guide can furthest mislead. Even the keenest writers commerce in clichés, false hypotheses, erring generalization, and confused metaphors. Like ordinary people, they adapt and even enslave reality to their whims, ideologies, and sensibilities. None entirely avoid offering old falsehoods and tedious moralizing for insight and truth.

We must always ask whether any local writer actually writes of his purported subject. Often locales and even regions (not unlike nations or even entire civilizations) are mere fodder for a writer's common opinion and excessive claim for fame.

Every writer deserves an interlocutor. We must scrutinize the work of even the greatest. To take a single example, we must look skeptically at the work of Minnesota rural writer Sinclair Lewis. We must ask in the case of his *Main Street* how faithfully he depicted reality in "Gopher Prairie," modeled on his own hometown Sauk Centre. We must query whether its principal character, Carol Kennicot, is not, as others have suggested, a mere reincarnation of Flaubert's Madame Bovary. We must ask why Lewis, who perceived so much about the Yankee business families along Sauk Centre's Main Street, showed no sympathy for or understanding of the Germans who populated the countryside of his Stearns County home. Was he but another alienated nineteenth- and twentieth-century Western intellectual? In aspiring to write an American *Madame Bovary*, did he unwittingly spread Paris's literary hegemony over our conceptualization of the American Midwestern small town?

Suspicion should not exempt non-fiction writers, either. We should bombard regional historians and social scientists of all stripes with criticism. Why do amateur local historians almost uniformly fail to place their subject in a larger regional, national, and even international context, while their academic counterparts treat localities as mere fodder for generalization mills? Why do the former seem content endlessly to recite old facts and tired stories, while the latter make real places and people abstract pawns in their remote theoretical games? Why did traditional historians of the prairie treat settlement as a heroic tale of bold individuals without reference to the world-wide economic and political forces that permitted and defined settlement, while contemporaries often glorify Indian culture's connection to the buffalo, oblivious to the place of muskrats, berries, and other humble fare in securing Indian survival?

Regional knowledge of southwestern Minnesota is especially flawed by its ignorance of the transformation of the contemporary countryside. The pervasive decline of population and quality of life on farm and in village, accented by two agricultural crises in two successive decades, must be fathomed. Turnover rates and demographic turbulence in rural lead cities in excess of those of metropolitan centers merit attention. The unprecedented transformation of the contemporary countryside must be grasped.

It is also imperative that historians, social scientists, and writers offer fresh perspectives and explanations of how rapidly prairie communities and cultures are vanishing. They must furnish us with innovative histories of agriculture, foods, gardens, diets, and lawns. They must tell the story of local bands, theaters, women's reading groups, baseball teams, dance halls, and fire departments. They must penetrate the inner side of changing local work, family life, pleasure, bathing, walking, leisure, and the honeymoon. They must explore the altered senses of the clandestine, and the successive waves of people who—initially considered illegal, marginal, and threatening—now populate our countryside.

At the same time there is need for inquiries into changing everyday rural life, altered regional sensibilities, and whole orders of transformed relationships. There is a nearly complete absence of contemporary histories of businesses, water use, and innovative materials, machines, and electronic technologies. Also profoundly welcomed would be histories of crops, of the mounting influence of world-wide markets, and of the steady intrusion of state laws and bureaucracies into the most remote corners of rural life. In sum, a multitude of changing microcosms challenge the contemporary regional scholar's mind.

This anthology offers part of our response to that summons. It also conveys our hope to stimulate bold and fresh stories about the place we call home. We would also like to believe that this book is in the best tradition of regional literature and rural studies practiced by our English Department and our Rural and Regional Studies Program, which Dave and I serve.

—Joseph Amato, January 26, 1999
Dean of Rural & Regional Studies

THE ANCIENT PEOPLE AND THE NEWLY COME

Born out of the caul of winter in the north, in the swing and circle of the horizon, I am rocked in the ancient land. As a child I first read the scriptures written on the scroll of frozen moisture by wolf and rabbit, by the ancient people and the newly come. In the beginning of the century the Indian smoke still mingled with ours. The frontier of the whites was violent, already injured by vast seizures and massacres. The winter nightmares of fear poisoned the plains nights with psychic airs of theft and utopia. The stolen wheat in the cathedrallike granaries cried out for vengeance.

Most of all one was born into space, into the great resonance of space, a magnetic midwestern valley through which the winds clashed in lassoes of thunder and lightning at the apex of the sky, the very wrath of God.

The body repeats the landscape. They are the source of each other and create each other. We were marked by the seasonal body of earth, by the terrible migrations of people, by the swift turn of a century, verging on change never before experienced on this greening planet. I sensed the mound and swell above the mother breast, and from embryonic eye took sustenance and benediction, and went from mother enclosure to prairie spheres curving into each other.

I was born in winter, the village snow darkened toward midnight, footsteps on boardwalks, the sound of horses pulling sleighs, and the ring of bells. The square wooden saltbox house held the tall shadows, thrown from kerosene lamps, of my grandmother and my aunt and uncle (missionaries home from India) inquiring at the door.

It was in the old old night of the North Country. The time of wood before metal. Contracted in cold, I lay in the prairie curves of my mother, in the planetary belly, and outside the vast horizon of the plains, swinging dark and thicketed, circle within circle. The round moon sinister reversed upside down in the sign of Neptune, and the twin fishes of Pisces swimming toward Aquarius in the dark.

But the house was New England square, four rooms upstairs and four rooms downstairs, exactly set upon a firm puritan foundation, surveyed on a level, set angles of the old geometry, and thrust up on the plains like an insult, a declamation of the conqueror, a fortress of our God, a shield against excess and sin.

I had been conceived in the riotous summer and fattened on light and stars that fell on my underground roots, and every herb, corn plant, cricket, beaver, red fox leaped in me in the old Indian dark. I saw everything was moving and entering. The rocking of mother and prairie breast curved around me within the square. The field crows flew in my flesh and cawed in my dream.

Crouching together on Indian land in the long winters, we grew in sight and understanding, heard the rumbling of glacial moraines, clung to the edge of holocaust forest fires, below-zero weather, grasshopper plagues, sin, wars, crop failures, drouth, and the mortgage. The severity of the seasons and the strangeness of a new land, with those whose land had been seized looking in our windows, created a tension of guilt and a tightening of sin. We were often snowed in, the villages invisible and inaccessible in cliffs of snow. People froze following the rope to their barns to feed the cattle. But the cyclic renewal and strength of the old prairie earth, held sacred by thousands of years of Indian ritual, the guerrilla soil of the Americas, taught and nourished us.

We flowed through and into the land, often evicted, drouthed out, pushed west. Some were beckoned to regions of gold, space like a mirage throwing up pictures of utopias, wealth, and villages of brotherhood. Thousands passed through the villages, leaving their dead, deposits of sorrow and calcium, leaching the soil, creating and marking with their faces new wheat and corn, producing idiots, mystics, prophets, and inventors. Or, as an old farmer said, we couldn't move; nailed to the barn door by the wind, we have to make a windmill, figure out how to plow without a horse, and invent barbed wire. A Dakota priest said to me, "It will be from here that the prophets come."

2

THE COUNTRYSIDE AS QUILT

In southwestern Minnesota, the countryside can be thought of as a quilt.

Each grove holds a different people, a different homestead, which can be rich or poor, new or long-established. Or yet, the grove can hide an old abandoned farmhouse left to the rain, wind, and the occasional beer parties of teenagers. At the grove's edge there might remain only great, shiny, new metal bins, storing surplus from a large farm, standing guard over squirrel and fox, rusting, rotting stuff, telling of people past. (In particular, I think of one abandoned homestead along the road to the dying village of Echo. Even the deepest snows do not conceal the indentation of the old foundation. Somehow that basin, it seems to me, should contain all the memories that make one family different from every other family.)

Then there are sections and townships. People there can be split by rivers and roads, be divided between Republicans and Democrats, be at odds over farm organizations, hold entirely different ideas of the market, hoard and speculate for entirely different reasons, and argue over the worth of cooperation.

Some townships seem to radiate memories of the past—old machinery, old struggles—and others speak of agriculture as boom or bust, brothers trying to invent a twelve-hundred-acre family farm.

One township—Normania—is really a Norwegian township. People from it still have a noticeable accent. They still identify with its church and cemetery, whose melting limestone markers speak the language of the old country.

Another nearby township is a mixture. It's not the story of one church, one town, one elevator, one anything. It's not even the story, as small things often are, of the struggle of two families, two school boards, two townships. One sees an infinitely complex whole.

At the level of counties and regions, histories of ethnic groups are often found. Here is where the Norwegians came and lived for two or three generations until all of them had traded off their farms so that their sons and daughters could make their living in professions, with words taking the place of manual labor.

Here is where the German Catholics live. They will never let go of their land. They would not trade it for the chance to go to the city or

5

to college. Holding, improving and paying for the land are what is good and right for them.

Between the Norwegians, Germans, Danes, Dutch, and Poles live the Belgians. They are thrifty, committed to family, church and their land. Prosperity for them can be had only on their own territory. In a few more generations, some say, they will own all the land hereabouts.

Every country has different groups who think separately about getting married, having children, working, and passing on the land. Only those who don't know the countryside speak of it without reference to its peoples' different ethnicities.

Some counties, even though they are adjacent to one another, seem, from a certain perspective, to be as different as Norwegians and Belgians, hills and valleys, sloughs and lakes. For example, in southwestern Minnesota, Lincoln and Lyon Counties, although right next to each other, have a different topography, a different politics, a different ethnicity, a different way of life.

The more westerly of the two counties, Lincoln County, has a higher elevation than Lyon. It is much more hilly, has sandier soil, suffers more erosion, and consequently, it is less vegetated with far fewer corn and soybean fields. At certain points Lincoln County looks like Western range country, with its cattle spread out over a hilly range,

and its farmers sporting ten gallon hats, high-heeled boots, and sheepskin jackets with a couple of the top buttons left undone.

If the West begins where vegetation fights for water rather than for space, as some argue, then there is good reason to think that the West starts in Lincoln County, Minnesota.

One thing is for sure: the higher elevation gives Lincoln a colder climate than Lyon. It is as if it is located a hundred miles to the north of Lyon rather than a few miles to the west.

The consequences are many: poorer farming, less to sell on the market, fewer towns, once a later and smaller immigration of settlers, now a proportionately greater emigration, fewer social services, lower incomes, more poverty, and a much higher infant mortality rate.

Perhaps this explains why Lincoln County farmers strike one as more fervent in their support of farm organizations, as more in pain and anger when they talk about the death of the family farm and the injustice of the present economic system.

If I were to go on, I could suggest yet more complex and varying patterns of this small section of the great prairie where I live. But there is no need: the truth sought has already been suggested. From the window of an airplane or a passing car, one does not perceive the truly complex pattern of historical, economic, geographical, cultural, ethnic, familial, and personal patches. I think of the countryside as a quilt.

GREAT SNOWS

Watering the Horse

How strange to think of giving up all ambition!
Suddenly I see with such clear eyes
The white flake of snow
That has just fallen on the horse's mane.

—Robert Bly

It is sometimes mistakenly thought by city people that grown-ups don't love snow. They think only children who haven't got to shovel it love snow, or only people like the von Furstenburgs and their friends who get to go skiing in exotic places and will never backslope a roadside in all their lives: that is a mistake. The fact is that most country or small-town Minnesotans love snow. They relish snow in large inconvenient storms; they like the excesses of it, they like the threat of it, the endless work of it, the glamour of it.

Before a storm, Madison is full of people excitedly laying in food stocks for the three-day blow. People lay in rather celebratory food, too. Organic-food parents get chocolate for the children; weight watchers lay in macaroni and Sara Lee cakes; recently converted vegetarians backslide to T-bones. People hang around the large Super-Valu window and keep a tough squinty-eyed watch on the storm progress with a lot of gruff, sensible observations (just like Houston Control talking to the moon, very much on top of it all) like "Ja, we need this for spring moisture . . ." or "Ja, it doesn't look like letting up at all . . ." or "Ja, you can see where it's beginning to drift up behind the VFW." The plain pleasure of it is scarcely hidden.

That is before the storm. Then the town empties out as the farmers and their families take their stocks home before U.S. 75, Minnesota 40, and Lac qui Parle 19 close up. During the storm itself heroism is the routine attitude. I remember once when the phone was out, before all the telephone lines went underground, and the power was off, our neighbor came lightly in his huge pack boots across the drift top, high up from our house level, like an upright black ant, delicately choosing his footing over the hard-slung and paralyzed snow waves. He looked as if he were walking across a frozen North Atlantic. He had come over to see if we were O.K. It was before snowmobiles, at -40 degrees a welcome gesture.

Then right after a storm we all go back uptown because we have to see how the town has filled. The streets are walled ten and eleven feet high. If they had had underground parking ramps in the pyramids this is what they'd have looked like, white-painted, and we crawl between the neatly carved clean walls. The horrible snow buildup is a point of pride. In 1969 a fine thing happened: the county of Lac qui Parle imported a couple of gigantic snow-removal machines from Yellowstone Park. It cost several thousand dollars to get those monsters here; when they arrived our heavy, many-layered, crusted snow broke the machines—they couldn't handle it. With glittering eyes we sent them back to Yellowstone Park.

Snowdrifts in the bad years, as in 1969, force us to dump garbage and nonburnables ever nearer the house, until finally in March there is a semicircle of refuse nearly at the front door. Even the German shepherd lowers his standards; the snow around the doghouse entrance is unspeakable.

If one has any kind of luck one garners comfort from great weather, but if there is some anxious and unresolved part of one's inner life, snowfall and certainly snowboundness can make it worse. During the winter of 1968-69, the three doctors of our town prescribed between two and three times as much tranquilizing medicine as usual. And Robert Frost, despite being one of the best snow poets going, has an odd, recurring fretfulness about snow:

The woods are lovely, dark and deep,
But I have promises to keep

What promises? To whom? If we think about it, it sounds moralistic and self-denying—a moral showing-off in some way. The nervousness is stronger, though, in "Desert Places":

Snow falling and night falling fast, oh, fast
In a field I looked into going past,
And the ground almost covered smooth in snow,
But a few weeds and stubble showing last.

The woods around it have it—it is theirs.
All animals are smothered in their lairs.
I am too absent-spirited to count;
The loneliness includes me unawares.

I am struck by the malaise of the word *absent-spirited*. It must mean—this joy in snow or fretfulness in snow—that whatever is providential and coming to each of us from within is sped the faster by snowfall.

Being out in a blizzard is not lovely. Nature then feels worse than inimical; it feels simply impersonal. It isn't that, like some goddess in Homer, she wants to grab and freeze your body in her drifts; it is that you can be taken and still the wind will keep up its regular blizzard whine and nothing has made a difference. In February of 1969 the fuel men couldn't get through for weeks; one midnight my husband and I had to transfer oil from a drum behind an old shed to our house tank. We did this in cans, load after load, crawling on all fours and rolling in the ravines between the drifts. It had some nice moments: every ten minutes or so we'd meet behind the old shed, when one returned an empty can and the other was coming away with a full one,

and we'd crouch in the scoured place, leaning over the nasty, rusted, infuriatingly slow spigot of the oil tank there. Looking at each other, we saw we had that impersonal aspect of snow-covered people. It was peculiar to think that anyone behind those freezing, melting, refreezing eyebrows ever objected to an act of Congress or ever loved a summer woods or memorized the tenor to anything by Christopher Tye. Back inside, our job done, still cold and rough-spoken, still walking like bears, we studied the children in their beds.

To us in Minnesota a blizzard in itself is of no practical good, but it is interesting how useful blizzards can be. Ordinary snowfall, not moved into deep-packed areas by wind, runs off too quickly in the spring and can't be controlled for good use. The *Proceedings of the American Society of Civil Engineers* has essay after essay on uses of Rocky Mountain snowmelt. Twenty-five hundred years ago, and possibly even earlier, the Persians used deep-drifted snow for irrigation. They built their *qanats*. Qanats are brick-walled tunnels running from the snowfields of the Elburz and other mountain ranges of Iran to villages fifteen or twenty miles away. At a point in the mountains' water table still higher than the land level of the parched miles and miles to be irrigated, the arched brick tunnels were carefully sloped to keep the water moving. The "mother well" was 200 feet deep and deeper. These 22,000 tunnels (there were 30,000 in 1960 but 8,000 were not in working condition) had air shafts for fresh air and maintenance access every 50 to 60 yards. Darius took the qanat technique to Egypt in the 5th century B.C. Nothing could have been cultivated in three-fourths of the now-irrigated fields of Iran without the ancient qanats. Persia was the originator of melons, cucumbers, and pears.

This is just to give an idea of mankind's long use of heavily drifted snow. Since we don't *use* blizzards in western Minnesota, the question lingers: why the pleasure in great weather? As with children in thunderstorms, I think we all have a secret affair of long standing with the other face of things. Children want the parents and the police and the other irritating powers to have their measure taken; they want a change of justice; but it goes further: they have a secret affection for bad weather.

Storms, what is more, force us to look at nature closely, and that is never boring. All meetings of the Business Improvement Association and the Countryside Council and the play rehearsal committees stop in a blizzard. It is a help. Two things make nature lovely to people, I think: enforced, extended leisure in a natural place— which storms give us out here; and second, planning our own lives instead of just following along. The moment, for example, that someone finally decides not to take the promising job offered by Reserve Mining, for example, or the moment someone decides not to pad a travel-expense account at the Ramada is a moment in which ice and snow and bare trunks look better, less happenstance, less pointless.

C.S. Lewis goes very far: he claims that the fact that we all agree on what is meant by *good* or *holy* (that is, no one thinks robbery or despoiling the land or depriving the poor is good) indicates that goodness and holiness are actually a normal, planned part of our universe—perfectly natural to the species. He would not be surprised at all to see snow on a horse's mane all the better for having just worked out an ethical decision.

—Carol Bly

What the Country Man Knows by Heart

1.

Why he lives there he can't say.
Silence is the rule.

But he knows where to look
When his wife is lost. He knows
Where the fish that get away go
And how to bring them back.
He's learned about lures
And knows how deep the bottom is.

He has been lost and found.
Where he lives moss grows everywhere.
He's made his way home
The way gulls fly through fog,
Find where water turns to stone.

In country covered with trees
He can find the heartwood
That burns best.
He can find his wife in smoke.

He knows where to look for rain
And why the wives of city men
Can not stop dreaming of water.

2.

When loons laugh he does not;
He waits for what follows,
Feeling the meaning of animal speech
Crawl in the base of his brain.

But he knows there are no words
To answer the question the owl has kept
Asking all these years.

He knows a man alone
Will begin to talk to himself
And why at last he begins to answer.

3.

He would never say any of this.
He knows how often silence speaks
Better than words; he knows
Not to try to say as much.

But then he won't say either
How often he longs to break the rule,
How unspoken words writhe in his throat
And blood beats the walls of his heart.

—Barton Sutter

Going Out to Get the Mail

across this whole prairie
nothing
to stop the wind
that bends
everything that will bend
and dries and shakes
human structures to dust

in shifting patterns snow
snakes across the road
sweeping plowed fields clean
filling ditches
the wind
an army
driving everything before it

highway signs shudder at their posts

nothing stays the same
the horizon has gone
white
leaving me exposed
as a lightning rod

nothing to stop the sky's
bare-taloned drop
to cover me with white wings

coming back
swimming hard
almost drowning in this current
breath is a dry gasp
a burning in the nostrils

thick crows yell from the bare grove
and the snow
has nearly covered my tracks
over the broken field

—Nancy Paddock

THE GRASS ROOTS OF GREAT PLAINS HISTORY

The tallgrass prairie encountered by nineteenth century settlers in southwestern Minnesota was an obvious contrast to previously settled Great Lakes forested regions because of its grass-based vegetation and also its rare hydrology. The region had an abundance of "prairie potholes," small wetlands that looked insignificant compared to major lakes. In reality, however, the potholes sustain diverse ecosystems based on rich seed beds. The vegetation was quite adaptable, a combination of aquatic species geared toward periods of high water and mudflat species more suited to lower depth conditions resembling a marsh. The plant life has a history of alternating according to natural circumstances. The fluctuation in plant species in turn dictates the populations of birds and wildlife.

An equally fundamental part of the tallgrass prairie was its major grasses. The main types can grow by themselves or in mixed seed beds. Switchgrass, a name that reflects the sound of grass rustled by the wind, is recognized for its rounded branch like tips and open spreading seed heads. One of its counterparts, Indian grass, has feathered seed heads clustered in a plume-like pinnacle. A third widespread grass species, Big Bluestem, is characterized by a three branched seed head that resembles a turkey's foot.

Most tallgrass vegetation is perennial and creates a natural shelter for wildlife. At the same time it offers a high yielding, high quality food source. The switchgrass and bluestem are regarded as sod-forming grasses because of their extensive, highly adaptable root systems.

Prairies experienced natural cycles of death and rebirth because of lightning-induced fires, most frequent in the spring and fall. Fire also became a tool for Native American societies. Planned fires offered insect control, easier day-to-day travel, and safe perimeters around encampments. Perhaps most importantly, fire-cleared areas were ideal for hunting large game, the traditional Great Plains livelihood.

Rebirth came about by natural processes, as wildfires reduced the build-up of organic materials and suppressed the encroachment of tree and shrub species that could crowd out vegetation. At the same time, soil nutrients such as nitrogen, potassium, phosphate and trace minerals naturally replenished themselves. Grass stands were free to grow back healthier than they'd been before a fire. Within a few days, new chutes sprang up amidst the scorched vegetation.

In their first treks across tallgrass prairie, explorers adopted the strategy used by Native Americans, threading their way along natural paths such as ridge tops or the edges of valleys. The routes were most clearly marked by signs of buffalo movement, making buffalo the region's earliest expedition guides.

The vastness of untamed Midwestern grassland is apparent by the value 19th-century newcomers placed on the region's few non-prairie locales, nearly the same value that desert travelers place on an oasis. In the mid-1830s, fur trader Joseph LaFramboise chose Minnesota's southern and westernmost maple basswood forest near present-day Lynd as the headquarters of his American Fur Company trading activities. The woods were already home to an abundance of fur-bearing wildlife and well-established Native American villages. Lynd is one in a group of Midwestern towns that is still nicknamed an "oasis on the prairie." The phrase sums up qualities that Native Americans and early settlers weren't likely to find out on the open grasslands, such as food, shade, sturdy shelter and free flowing spring water.

As economic activity branched out from the sheltered valleys, native grasslands steadily yielded to plows. Tethered oxen and horses paced across fields once the domain of wildlife. Most original prairie remnants, less than one percent of the estimated 18 million acres in Southwestern Minnesota, exist along hillsides in areas nobody wished to cultivate.

Prairie pothole wetlands saw a similar fate, as an estimated 80 percent were drained across Minnesota's farm belt. In Nobles County near the southern and western Minnesota borders only about 1,000 out of 137,000 pre-settlement wetland acres remain undisturbed. The earliest water management boards were sometimes known as "drain boards," reflecting the drive toward elaborate networks of drainage tile.

Meanwhile, organized settlement pushed westward into the drier and less hospitable shortgrass prairie stretching from the Dakota Territory to the Texas panhandle, which represented a final frontier for the Midwestern farm belt. It possessed shorter, less varied grasses, an indication that it would be equally restrictive with field crops.

However, population maps of the twentieth-century Midwest show that, for the most part, settlement patterns did not come close to what early developers envisioned. Rather than an evenly spaced and well populated farm region, settlement thinned out far short of the Rocky Mountains. Western edges of the farm belt were left with fewer towns, more distance between regional centers, and less population density in the countryside. To local residents and national observers alike, it kept a Western identity. It had its own cattle and wheat economy rather than an imitation of the central corn belt.

The abrupt end of westward corn belt expansion challenged the notion of continuous growth, opening the door for self-doubt in the Dust Bowl era of the 1930s. As untamed grass symbolized opportunity, uncontrolled drought suggested the Plains were a deficient region. The image remained in the more prosperous post-war era of the 1950s, when the agricultural heartland missed out on much of the economic boom that took shape on the Eastern Seaboard, the West Coast and urban parts of the Great Lakes region.

As a result, a high percentage of young people became convinced that they had to leave the prairie region in order to succeed, leaving behind small family farms and community schools. In some respects, their desire to leave was as powerful as the desire of their ancestors to turn the prairie into a home. The exodus was documented in many of the best known cultural symbols, including *The Grapes of Wrath* and *The Wizard of Oz*.

Other less dramatic factors, however, were at work to keep the farm belt alive. One of the most significant was a shift from urban terminal stockyards. Wishing to ship animals for shorter distances, packers established processing plants in smaller Midwestern cities. With other farm-based businesses like grain elevators and creameries, they gave many regions a small yet significant industry, enough to create an economically vital source of wage-based income.

A second trend involved the soybean, produced mostly in China until World War II. Spurred by government price support limits on corn production and reduced demand for oats as machines replaced workhorses, soybeans became the region's second major cash crop in the 1940s. Minnesota production rose from one to ten million bushels per year in just six years.

The most recent farm innovations occurred alongside a modest resurgence of native grass and wetlands. Land retirement efforts such as the 1980s and 1990s Conservation Reserve Program, partly a response to historically low crop prices, grew to encompass more than two million acres in Minnesota. They thereby went more than ten percent of the way toward the original tallgrass landscape. Pipestone National Monument is in its third decade of planned prairie burns, a scaled-down and controlled version of historic wildfires.

The surest prediction for the future is that life on the prairie will remain intertwined with the land. It means a risk of drought and floods, a hope for bumper crops, and a reputation for stability that somehow defies natural extremes. Even though some people stay, and some people leave, some people return and others come for the first time, spring occurs once each year and time marches on. The grass roots history continues.

—Jim Muchlinski

ON THE COTEAU DES PRAIRIES, 1838

THURSDAY, JUNE 28,1838. Nothing equals the purity and the elasticity of the air we breathe, but the wind blows constantly because nothing interrupts its movement. It is a new world which will be at the disposal of the people of later centuries, when the forests will come to restore the flow of the meteorological agents and modify the harshness of the climate by tempering the fury of the winds. We have observed for several days that the rain falls frequently in faraway regions and does not reach us; only several drops of rain from the storms that pass at a distance fall on our tents in the rapid passage of the clouds that rush toward the wooded country without stopping above the prairies. We believe ourselves favored by heaven because an almost constantly serene sky and pure air accompany us, but we see also that Providence makes us feel the effects of the barbarity of man in depriving us of water, a natural consequence of the destruction of the forests. Summing up, wherever the annual fires have not reached, there remains the evidence of forests which existed in another time.

After having left the Great Oasis behind—although our route continues to cross the bare prairies without landmarks—the prospect changes and becomes more cheerful, more varied due to the undulating surface of the ground that presents before us summits which are lost in the mists of the horizon, making us believe in high mountains far away that, however, sink back to the general level of the ground as we approach. Nothing is more difficult than to judge distances. One distinguishes at a considerable distance the least little projection, or the littlest object which appears accidentally on these crests so clear and distinct, that thrusts up against the sky. It is often an illusion similar to that which makes the moon look larger on the horizon than toward the zenith. Many times our dogs seen on the crests in front of us appear as big as horses. At other times, crests far away seem to us to be very near. This takes place especially when the shadows of several clouds pass between us and these crests, and as the clouds move always very rapidly, we see the crest recede into the distance at the same speed the cloud recedes and vanishes.

Toward 8:45 we found ourselves at the sources of the Des Moines River. It trickles here at the bottom of a pretty vale in a rivulet that comes from a lake, or rather from a muskeg pond *[Klinkers Marsh]*, having entered this lake from another even smaller *[Lange Marsh]*, which is the last, situated higher 4 miles to the NW of the first. Between these two lakes the river gains another stream on its right, coming from a coulee at the head of which the waters of this stream flow from a little marsh or little lake on the dividing ridge of the Mississippi and the Missouri—a typical case. We stop at the foot of the lake where our route crosses the river. We lunch and I take a geographical position.

At 3:00 we leave the station and continue our route across the same sort of landscape that had charmed us this morning. Each time that we arrive on the summit of an undulation, we stop to contemplate its general effect and that of the country we are leaving and which opens up before us.

Here I observe to be still more evident a fact that has attracted my attention for several days: The traces of a great primitive deposit always accompanying us and showing itself from time to time on the slopes of the valleys in considerable masses. But one sees further some rocks that could be the geological formation that is the foundation of the regions we are crossing. This formation is hidden by the deposits of primitive and transitional rocks, accumulated in such prodigious quantity that they are the cause of the undulating form and the changing level of the ground. Wherever there are some outlines or angles jutting from the tops of the crests, a little exposed by the furious action of the northwest wind that rules here three-quarters of the year, the soil is torn away, carried afar, leaving the accumulated material laid bare. It is always granite of various kinds that dominates.

The Sioux use these rolled stones and massed materials laid bare on the highest summits to make signals. Sometimes these are in conical pyramids. Sometimes they cover the tomb of those who died traveling across the prairies and who want to be buried on the high places. Sometimes the Sioux have amused themselves by making fantastic objects. They give names to these localities, which thus serve as landmarks in a country where there are no other geographical beacons.

Toward 5:00 we reach the crest of the highest elevation that we have seen and that we can see in this region. It is the one that separates the water of the Mississippi from that of the Missouri, the highest location on this great plateau with all its undulating crests.

The direction of this high Coteau is generally SE to NW. Where we cross it, the crest is formed by two coteaux between which one finds marshes, one of which supplies water to the little stream that flows between the two lakes at the source of the Des Moines of which I spoke earlier. Following for 8 or 9 miles the southeastern spur of the principal Coteau dividing the Mississippi and the Missouri, I find a pond, a marsh, a muskeg, or an elastic prairie from which a little river flows into *Riviere du Rocher [Rock River],* one of the upper tributaries of the Missouri whose source we immediately discover in descending the other side of the Coteau. This little river *[Chanarambie Creek]* follows a deep ravine, its sides wooded since they are protected against fire. But the tops of these trees are not visible above the level of the prairie, and as wood is so rare, knowledge of it is precious; the Sioux name this *tchan narhambedan*—the hidden wood.

The same marsh of which we just spoke supplies, when the water is high, a little trickle that falls into the Des Moines River. This marsh is called by the Sioux *Okshida nom Witcha Ktepi*—the place where the young men were killed (by the Sauk). The Rock

River takes its name from a little hill that is on the right bank, about halfway along its course, below a detour which it makes after it has been joined by Chanarambie Creek. It is named, because of that circumstance, *iyan heaka watpa*—river of the stone hill. Almost opposite this rock enters *la Riviere du Bois Piquant [Champepadan Creek]*, the *tchan pepedan watpa [thorny wood]* of the Sioux, and farther down on the same side, the left bank of the Rock River, enters the *kanrhanzi witcha ktepi [Kanaranzi Creek]*—or the river where the Kansas were killed. *Kanhanzi* is the Sioux name for Kansas.

Finally I will add as an explanation of what I have said above on the customs of the Sioux that to the east of the marsh and on the crest of the principal Coteau that passes beside it I find a summit where the primitive deposit was uncovered. The Sioux, one does not know when, brought together the stones of the place and made with them a representation of a man and named the place *iyan Witchashta Karhapi*—the place where they have made a man of stone.

Hardly had we begun to descend the southeast slope of the principal Coteau when we discovered, in the distance to our right, the coulees from which the Rock River gathers water; the sources consist of two main branches *[East and West Rock River]*. At 6:00 we arrive on the bank of the first *[East Rock]* which is also the shorter. There remained still 3 or 4 miles to go to reach the second *[West Rock]*, and I was anxious to reach it. But two incidents obliged us to set to work without delay on our encampment for the night. First, the rain that had been threatening us for several hours, falling from a storm cloud on the horizon while we were having the most beautiful weather in the world; second, the signs of smoke that we had seen the day before and that we had seen again from the top of the principal Coteau, but that this time have to be at no more than 10 or 12 miles, some two days' march from the distance we supposed them the first time. The Sauk and the Fox were not, then, far away. They were able to see us, and thus we might fear their nocturnal visit and fear for our horses and our young Sioux and our two Sioux young women. If this is a party of young men, they have seen the flag of the United States; but if there is a chief at the head of it, they will come visiting in friendship, and while I shall be listening to the friendly harangue of the chief, the young men will slaughter my dear hosts.

We put our arms in good shape, I double the night guard, and we pass a good tranquil night at the bottom of the coulee where we cower beside the stream that I just spoke of, and that furnishes us pure water, fresh and having a slight taste of niter. We were not visited by the rain or by the Sauk and Fox. Route of the day. From the Great Oasis to the encampment for lunch on the Des Moines River—6 miles. From there to the principal Coteau—5 miles. From there to the first fork of the sources of the Rock River—2 1/2 miles. Total—13 1/2 miles. Our marching days are not long, but they cannot be when one occupies the time as we do.

—Joseph N. Nicollet

HORIZONTAL GRANDEUR

For years I carried on a not-so-jovial argument with several friends who are north-woods types. They carted me out into the forests of northern Wisconsin or Minnesota, and expected me to exclaim enthusiastically on the splendid landscape. "Looks fine," I'd say, "but there's too damn many trees, and they're all alike. If they'd cut down twenty miles or so on either side of the road, the flowers could grow, you could see the sky and find out what the real scenery is like." Invariably, this provoked groans of disbelief that anyone could be insensitive enough to prefer dry, harsh, treeless prairies. There, a man is the tallest thing for miles around; a few lonesome cottonwoods stand with leaves shivering by a muddy creek; sky is large and readable as a Bible for the blind. The old farmers say you can see weather coming at you, not like woods, where it sneaks up and takes you by surprise.

I was raised in Minneota, true prairie country. When settlers arrived in the 1870s they found waist-high grass studded with wild flowers; the only trees were wavy lines of cottonwoods and willows along the crooked Yellow Medicine Creek. Farmers emigrated here not for scenery, but for topsoil; 160 flat acres without trees or

boulders to break plows and cramp fields was beautiful to them. They left Norway, with its picturesque but small, poor, steep farms; or Iceland, where the beautiful backyard mountains frequently covered hay fields with lava and volcanic ash. Wives, described by Ole Rolvaag in *Giants in the Earth*, were not enamored with the beauty of black topsoil, and frequently went insane from loneliness, finding nowhere to hide on these blizzardy plains. But the beauty of this landscape existed in function, rather than form, not only for immigrant farmers, but for Indians who preceded them.

Blackfeet Indians live on the Rocky Mountains' east edge in northern Montana—next to Glacier National Park. Plains were home for men and buffalo, the source of Blackfeet life; mountains were for feasting and dancing, sacred visions and ceremonies, but home only for spirits and outlaws. It puzzles tourists winding up hairpin turns, looking down three thousand feet into dense forests on the McDonald Valley floor, that Blackfeet never lived there. It did not puzzle the old farmer from Minneota who, after living and farming on prairies most of his life, vacationed in the Rockies with his children after he retired. When they reached the big stone escarpment sticking up at the prairie's edge, one of his sons asked him how he liked the view. "These are

stone," the old man said; "I have stones in the north eighty. These are bigger, and harder to plow around. Let's go home."

When my mother saw the Atlantic Ocean in Virginia, she commented that though saltier, noisier, and probably somewhat larger, it was no wetter or more picturesque than Dead Coon Lake or the Yellow Medicine River and surely a good deal more trouble to cross.

There are two eyes in the human head—the eye of mystery, and the eye of harsh truth—the hidden and the open—the woods eye and the prairie eye. The prairie eye looks for distance, clarity, and light; the woods eye for closeness, complexity, and darkness. The prairie eye looks for usefulness and plainness in art and architecture; the woods eye for the baroque and ornamental. Dark old brownstones on Summit Avenue were created by a woods eye; the square white farmhouse and red barn are prairie eye's work. Sherwood Anderson wrote his stories with a prairie eye, plain and awkward, told in the voice of a man almost embarrassed to be telling them, but bullheadedly persistent to get at the meaning of the events; Faulkner, whose endless complications of motive and language take the reader miles behind the simple facts of an event, sees the world with a

woods eye. One eye is not superior to the other, but they are different. To some degree, like male and female, darkness and light, they exist in all human heads, but one or the other seems dominant. The Manicheans were not entirely wrong.

I have a prairie eye. Dense woods or mountain valleys make me nervous. After once visiting Burntside Lake north of Ely for a week, I felt a fierce longing to be out. Driving home in the middle of the night, I stopped the car south of Willmar, when woods finally fell away and plains opened up. It was a clear night, lit by a brilliant moon turning blowing grasses silver. I saw for miles—endless strings of yard lights, stars fallen into the grove tops. Alone, I began singing at the top of my voice. I hope neither neighborhood cows, nor the Kandiyohi County sheriff was disturbed by this unseemly behavior from a grown man. It was simply cataracts removed from the prairie eye with a joyful rush.

Keep two facts in mind if you do not have a prairie eye: magnitude and delicacy. The prairie is endless! After the South Dakota border, it goes west for over a thousand miles, flat, dry, empty, lit by brilliant sunsets and geometric beauty. Prairies, like mountains, stagger the imagination most not in detail, but size. As a mountain is high, a prairie is wide; horizontal grandeur, not vertical. People neglect prairies as scenery because they require time and patience to comprehend. You eye a mountain, even a range, at a glance. The ocean spits and foams at its edge. You see down into the Grand Canyon. But walking the whole prairie might require months. Even in a car at 60 miles an hour it takes three days or more. Like a long symphony by Bruckner or Mahler, prairie unfolds gradually, reveals itself a mile at a time, and only when you finish crossing it do you have any idea of what you've seen. Americans don't like prairies as scenery or for national parks and preserves because they require patience and effort. We want instant gratification in scenic splendor as in most things, and simply will not look at them seriously. Prairies are to Rockies what *Paradise Lost* is to haiku. Milton is cumulative; so are prairies. Bored for days, you are suddenly struck by the magnitude of what has been working on you. It's something like knowing a woman for years before realizing that you are in love with her after all.

If prairie size moves the imagination, delicacy moves the heart. West of Minneota, the prairies quickly rise several hundred feet and form the Coteau. This land looks more like the high plains of Wyoming. Rougher and stonier than land to the east, many sections

have never been plowed. Past Hendricks, along the south and west lake shores, things open up—treeless hills with grazing cattle, gullies with a few trees sliding off toward the lake. Ditches and hillsides are a jumble of flowers, grasses and thistles: purple, pink, white, yellow, blue. In deep woods, the eye misses these incredible delicate colors, washed in light and shadow by an oversized sky. In the monochromatic woods, light comes squiggling through onto a black green shadowy forest floor. My eye longs for a rose, even a sow thistle.

A woods man looks at twenty miles of prairie and sees nothing but grass, but a prairie man looks at a square foot and sees a universe; ten or twenty flowers and grasses, heights, heads, colors, shades, configura-tions, bearded, rough, smooth, simple, elegant. When a cloud passes over the sun, colors shift, like a child's kaleidoscope.

I stop by a roadside west of Hendricks, walk into the ditch, pick a prairie rose. This wild pink rose is far lovelier than hot-house roses wrapped in crinkly paper that teenagers buy prom dates. The dusty car fills with its smell. I ignore it for a few minutes, go on talking. When I look again, it's dry, as if pressed in an immigrant Bible for a hundred years. These prairie flowers die quickly when you take them out of their own ground. They too are immigrants who can't transplant, and wither fast in their new world.

I didn't always love prairies. On my father's farm I dreamed of traveling, living by the sea and, most of all, close to mountains. As a boy, I lay head on a stone in the cow pasture east of the house, looking up at cloud rows in the west, imagining I saw all the way to the Rockies and that white tips on the clouds were snow on mountaintops or, better yet, white hair on sleeping blue elephant spines. Living in a flat landscape drove me to indulge in mountainous metaphor, then later discover that reality lived up to it. When I finally saw the Rockies years later, they looked like pasture clouds, phantasmagorias solider than stone.

The most astonished travelers do not come from the Swiss Alps, or the California coast. Only William Carlos Williams, who lived in the industrial prairies of New Jersey, would notice the Mexico of *Desert Music*. A southwest poet with a wood's eye would have seen sequaro cactus or medieval parapets. Trust a prairie eye to find beauty and understate it truthfully, no matter how violent the apparent exaggeration. Thoreau, though a woodsman, said it right: "I can never exaggerate enough."

—Bill Holm

32

Picking Rock

Renters pick fast and loose;
if you own the land, you pick close.

You can pick the field clean one year,
come back the next, and find more.

They rise up from somewhere far below.
Just how far, I don't know.

It's a rain,
but slow, and upside down.

The higher up you get,
like this tractor seat,
the easier they are to spot.

Sometimes I think there are
pregnant ones down there.

Most are granite, some are limestone.
This is no work for one person alone.

There's one kind, blue-black,
that's twice as heavy as it looks.

This one looks like a brain.
Somebody was thinking too hard again.

Here's an old Indian hammerhead.
You can see where the leather strap fitted.

Sometimes it seems everywhere you look
there's a rock.

—Philip Dacey

33

BONES

I was never confined as a child in Chippewa County, Minnesota, to any space so constricted as a house. Of course our family had a house, or a succession of them, that I shared: first a cement-block basement house, then a balloon-frame shack, finally an honest, full-fledged farmhouse with rooms and staircases and a real basement and rag rugs on the linoleum floors. But none of these houses fully contained the place where I lived. In the country one lives not in a house but on a farm and thinks of the space one occupies as including everything within its fence lines. But for me, something more was at work. In our little country church I heard often the promise of heaven. I visualized it not as cloudy and ethereal but as a concrete place, according to the words of Jesus: "In my father's house are many mansions." I thought of my own Minnesota home as a smaller version of heaven, as a house of many mansions. There was the wooden-frame house with the green mansard roof where I slept and ate and joined the life of the family. But it was only one of my many mansions.

I lived, for one thing, in the hayloft where I stored my collection of bones. When it was too stormy to be outside, I was likely to spend the day there, swinging from the ropes or standing in the crow's nest at the peak of the gables where I could see out across the river valley through a little round window. I kept company with the pigeons, read, napped in a bed of hay, teased spiders out of their chambers, daydreamed.

And I lived with squirrels and pale tree frogs in the limbs of an enormous black walnut tree at the far end of the pasture. It was always shady there, and a fresh breeze always seemed, even in the stillest and hottest weather, to be blowing around that tree. Its limbs were broad enough to lie down upon, as I often did, listening to the murmur of summer afternoons, the buzzing of flies, the droning of bumblebees, the singing of birds. Near it were the hollow of a pioneer's sod hut and a sweet-water spring that ran all winter. I imagined that the sod house was mine in the making, that the spring had drawn me there, and that I would live forever in the shadow of the wide arms of the walnut tree.

I lived also along the shores of the pasture pond, where the pussy willows swelled in the springtime; and blackbirds wheezed and wheedled in the cattails; and muskrats swam in the musty, warm summer waters, green with algae and duckweed. I lived among the arrowroots and jewelweeds, among the strawberries hiding in the

cordgrass, among minks, weasels, and fat skunks. Water striders and boatmen and pill bugs squatted in my front yard, right-handed pond snails and leopard frogs in my backyard, dragonflies and damselflies in the fetid air overhead. I passed many happy hours in the upper reaches of a black willow tree, monitoring the progress of life in the fecund chambers of my pond mansion.

And I lived by the blue light of the moon along country lanes so quiet I could hear the town traffic miles away, visible only as a burst of mysterious light on the distant horizon. Fireflies flashed in the road ditches, and long leaves of corn sighed in the evening breezes. Here and there a dog barked in a farmyard. The sound of dogs barking in the night, of their barks echoing across the vast, empty countryside, was the surfacing sound of the wildness in them. I could hear in their voices the ancient cries of gray wolves in the days when great herds of bison roamed the plains and the moonlight danced in the endless waves of grass. I could feel then the wildness in my own bones.

And I lived in a woodpile, in a plum thicket, in the striped shade of an August cornfield, where the whirligigs raced across the sweltering landscape, showering dust like rain. And in a prairie meadow, among overgrazed river bluffs, on a granite island in a widening of the river, along a grassy fenceline where a lone green ash grew.

Again, I lived along the riverbanks where beaver built their dams; mud turtles sunned on half-submerged logs; bullheads and northern pike, saugers and buffalo fish swam the murky waters; white-tailed deer came down to drink; the tracks of mink mingled in the shoreline mud with the remains of the deer-toe clams they had fished from the shallows.

But mainly I dwelled along the river under the spell of its mysterious waters, which ran to the Minnesota River, then into the Mississippi River, then down the central nervous cord of the continent, over the plains of Iowa, through the hills of Missouri and Arkansas, across the bayous of Louisiana, and into the Gulf of Mexico.

In my house there were many mansions.

When I sat on the overhanging limb of a willow tree dangling my bare feet into the brown Chippewa River, feeling the slow, steady tug of its unfailing current against my toes, I became connected to the great body of the continent. I was linked not merely with a small river in western Minnesota but swept up into the gigantic stream of life. I lived then in the piney waters of the North Woods, in the thundering waters of St. Anthony Falls, in the icy rush of mountain streams, in the stagnant backwaters of southern marshes, in the oceanic brine. I shared then a mansion with my little bullheads, yes, but also with ancient paddlefishes and cutthroat trout and sharks and catfishes as big as logs. I lived then among bald eagles and alligators and panthers. I lived where it always snows and where it never snows, high in the mountains and at the edge of the sea.

As a high school biology student, I once traced the cardio-vascular system of a domestic cat whose blood vessels had been injected with a rubbery substance, blue for the veins, red for the arteries. Beginning at the heart, I traced the vessels up into its skull and down into its toes and out along its tail, following them as they branched into smaller and smaller streams. It was an ecstatic experience; I carried my half-excavated specimen home in a clear plastic bag, unable to bear the suspense of waiting until the next day's class to discover where all the vessels ran. No one would sit in the same bus seat with me, but I was too excited to mind. There in the body of the cat lay a map of the world as I perceived it from my vantage point along the Chippewa River. I might be one tiny red corpuscle swimming in the slenderest of the tail arteries, but I was an undeniable part of something big and alive, a constituent particle of the whole organism. I had seen the universe in a two-dollar laboratory specimen.

—Paul Gruchow

THE FIRST PEOPLES OF SOUTHWESTERN MINNESOTA

We all know that the southwestern Minnesota of today is very different from that of 150 years ago. When the region was settled by Euro-Americans after the Civil War, prairie grasses covered the ground for as far as the eye could see. Innumerable shallow lakes and sloughs dotted the landscape, making overland travel difficult. Turgid rivers wound through the endless prairie, in and out of the muskrat sloughs towards a final whitewater plunge into the valley of the Minnesota River. Government land surveyors heaped up the bison bones that littered the ground for section markers because, as witnesses attest, trees were scarce. Dakota Indians could still be seen, but the memories of 1862 had stripped any romantic notions of noble savages.

Over the last century and a half we have greatly changed the land. The patchwork quilt of agricultural fields is divided by towns, roads, fencelines, and farm groves. Most of the lakes and sloughs have been drained and their rich bottoms are now plowed. The rivers have been dammed and straightened. The bison and their bones have disappeared. When one thinks of Indians, it is Jackpot Junction Casino that first comes to mind.

As the southwestern Minnesota of today is very different from that of the first white settlers, the southwestern Minnesota of 150 years ago was very different from that of the first human settlers. Indian history began 12,000 years ago in Minnesota. It began when warm, dry winds started to melt the glaciers and the grey rock-strewn landscape began to turn green.

People of the Dark Forest

An open spruce forest first reclaimed the rocky soil left by the glaciers. This forest gradually filled in to become a full-fledged boreal forest, dark and dense like the forest of *Peter and the Wolf*. People had entered North America from northeastern Asia during the glacial maximum when sea level had dropped almost 300 feet. This formed a land bridge across the Bering Sea connecting Alaska with Asia. These first immigrants were trapped in Alaska until the glaciers began to recede and an ice-free corridor opened to the east side of the Rocky Mountains. Down this corridor small bands of hunters wandered into the virgin wilderness of America.

Some of these groups of hunters were the first people to enter southwestern Minnesota. Compared to the grasslands of the southern Plains and the open deciduous forests of the southeastern United States, southwestern Minnesota was not an especially inviting place to live. The dense boreal forest was not rich in game. The Minnesota River Valley was filled with a torrent known as Glacial River Warren, the only outlet to massive Lake Agassiz. River Warren made travel between westcentral and southwestern Minnesota almost impossible. Melting blocks of ice buried in the glacial gravels made the landscape unstable. The mass of the glacier still in northern Minnesota made the summers cool and the winters bitterly cold.

The first people of southwestern Minnesota hunted mastodon and giant beaver with spears tipped with beautifully made stone points. These points were long and lean with a large flake scar at the bottom called a "flute." These earliest fluted points are very rare with only a few found in all of Minnesota. These people are related to the mammoth and bison hunters of the southern Plain. Archaeologists call them "Clovis" people, because one of their campsites was first discovered near Clovis, New Mexico.

As the climate continued to get warmer and drier, deciduous trees invaded the spruce forest. By 10,000 years ago, an oak-elm forest covered all of southwestern Minnesota. Many large animals like mammoth and mastodon became extinct. A new kind of projectile point technology replaced the Clovis points. The new spearheads, which first appear in the southern Plains about 11,000 years ago, are called Folsom points. Folsom points are usually smaller than Clovis points and they have a flute scar that runs almost the entire face of the points.

Folsom points have been found in plowed fields in a few southwestern Minnesota counties. The Cottonwood River area in Brown County has yielded several Folsom points. Folsom people were

much like Clovis people in their daily lives. They never stayed in one place very long. As forests became more open, more animals were available to hunt and more plant foods were available to gather.

There were never many Clovis and Folsom people in southwestern Minnesota. For the first two thousand years of human occupation, no more than one hundred people at any one time may have been present. Most of the archaeological remains they left behind have been deeply buried by collapsing river valleys and floods and gradual soil development. These first people will always remain mysterious even when archaeologists finally find one of their campsites in relatively good condition. Scattered bones may attest to the animals they hunted and stone tools will give us a glimpse of their technology, but we will never know their gods or their language or the way they treated each other.

People of the Endless Prairie

By 9,500 years ago, prairie began to displace the oak-elm forest in southwestern Minnesota. Within 500 years this prairie covered all of the region. Southwestern Minnesota looked like it looked to the first European explorers, with one major difference: the bison herds which roamed these ancient prairies were not modern bison, but a now-extinct form that was much more massive.

The people who hunted these bison no longer used fluted points. The points were still lanceolate in shape, however, and very finely made. A burial of one these bison hunters was found in a gravel pit in Browns Valley in the 1930s. He had been buried with several of his spearheads in a pit dug into the gravel. His body had been stained with red ochre.

These early bison hunters had many different projectile point styles. The Browns Valley points are of a style that is not widespread in the Upper Midwest. Other point styles found in southwestern Minnesota have been found throughout the Great Plains. Unlike the fluted points of the first people, almost every county in southwestern Minnesota has yielded spear-heads from these early bison hunters.

The daily lives of these bison hunters were similar to the Clovis and Folsom peoples, although wild foods may have been more plentiful and campsites more permanent. The lakes and rivers would have been full of fish and with the retreat of the glaciers into central Canada, migratory waterfowl began to establish patterns that they still follow today. Plant foods would have been abundant in the shallow lakes.

As the post-glacial warming and drying continued, the prairie moved to the north and east. By 7,000 years ago, at the peak of this climatic trend, grassland covered all of Minnesota except the far northeast. Itasca Park was a prairie and the Mississippi River wound through prairie for its entire length in Minnesota. The warming and drying had a devastating affect on southwestern Minnesota. We know how severe the droughts of the 1930s were. Imagine a period of drought more frequent and more severe lasting for centuries. Between 8,000 and 5,000 years ago, droughts ravaged southwestern Minnesota. Most of the lakes may have been dry most of the time. Many of the rivers did not flow. Ducks, fish, and aquatic mammals were rare. Prairie fires blackened the land.

But this dry period does not mean southwestern Minnesota was abandoned by people. Much the opposite. As the prairie expanded, so too did the bison herds. Southwestern Minnesota had massive bison herds rivaling the herds of the central Great Plains encountered by later Europeans.

As other resources disappeared, people became much more focused on bison hunting. A way of life developed that continued on the Great Plains up until the European invasion destroyed the bison

herds in the mid-19th century. Bison hunting dominated the lives of the people of southwestern Minnesota for thousands of years even though hunting technology changed. Projectile points became shorter, less finely made, and they had notches near the base. New forms of tools were introduced, making the preparation of vegetal foods easier. Dogs were domesticated. House forms changed. But one thing remained constant: the bison.

People of the Island Lakes

By 5,000 years ago, the climate in the Upper Midwest had settled into its modern pattern. Droughts still occurred, but they were not as frequent or as intense. The prairie retreated to the boundaries that would last until Euro-American settlement. Lakes were full of water most of the time. Fish and geese and muskrats returned. Bison remained, but the very large herds moved west.

As the climate settled down, so too did people. Islands and peninsulas in the shallow lakes became the favorite spots for villages. These locations were one of the few places in the prairie that had woods protected from prairie fires. They had the added benefits of being good defensive locations and easy access to the rich aquatic resources of the shallow lakes.

It is during this period that the people of southwestern Minnesota become different from their neighbors. Bison hunting was still very important to these people, but their economies diversified to meet the changes of the seasons and the local availability of food. When the bison herds left the area, they did not need to follow them to survive. They remained in their island villages, hunting muskrats, catching fish, and wading in the shallow waters to find the nutritious waterlily tubers.

In winter, times were tough and the villages split into smaller bands. Many of these bands moved into the larger river valleys where wood for fires was more plentiful, deer more common, and there was shelter from the cold north winds. Hunting forays onto the open prairie occasionally found small groups of bison. A successful hunt could avert starvation for months with one adult bison yielding one thousand pounds of edible meat.

About 2,500 years ago, a major technological innovation appeared in southwestern Minnesota. People began to make pottery. This allowed them to cook and store their food more easily. They developed a distinctive style of decoration which featured trailed lines near the vessel rims across surfaces that had been impressed with woven cord. This ceramic style was first noted by archaeologists digging on an island in Fox Lake near the town of Sherburn in Martin County. The pottery is now called Fox Lake, as are the people.

In other areas around the prairie lake region, people also began to bury their dead in earthen mounds at this time. But the Fox Lake people of southwestern Minnesota appear to have resisted the widespread practice of mound building. They saw the value of pottery, but their old ways of treating the dead were good enough. This may reflect the basic conservative nature of their culture. While groups around them developed more structured societies, Fox Lake people retained an egalitarian system where there was no need to note the special status of a leader upon his death.

Other technological changes took place about 1500 years ago. The bow and arrow appeared. Pottery became more globular, more thin-walled, and the trailed line decoration was abandoned in favor of cord-wrapped sticks. This type of pottery was first noted at an archaeological site on an island in Lake Benton in Lincoln County, giving both the pottery and its makers a name.

Lake Benton pottery resembles pottery found in central Minnesota. This suggests that Lake Benton people were in close contact with people outside of the prairie lake region. Burial mounds also appear in southwestern Minnesota at this time suggesting major societal changes, although the basic way of life remained unchanged.

People still built their villages on islands and peninsulas and the same animals appear to make up the diet.

People of the Fertile Valleys

Major change came to the prairie lake region about 1,000 years ago. These were not merely changes in technology, but changes in way of life. They were changes brought about not just by the spread of ideas, but the intrusion of new people, villagers who were more sedentary than the Lake Benton people and grew corn and other vegetables. These people partitioned southwestern Minnesota, and while they occasionally traded with each other, they also built their villages in locations where defense was a primary consideration. The villages were located in river valleys where soils in the floodplains are rich, well-watered, and easily tilled.

Along the Blue Earth River in Faribault and Blue Earth counties, several large horticultural village complexes were established at the junctions of major creeks such as Center Creek near Winnebago and Willow Creek near Vernon Center. The people in these villages made a distinctive type of pottery that is globular, smooth surfaced, and tempered with bits of ground up clamshell. The pottery is related to a widespread cultural complex in the Midwest which archaeologists call Oneota. Oneota peoples spoke Siouan languages and were related to modern day groups such as the Ioway, the Oto, and the Winnebago. The Oneota peoples of the eastern prairie lake region are called Blue Earth.

Blue Earth peoples lived in villages that may have had several hundred inhabitants. They grew corn and hunted deer. They also had far-flung hunting camps in the interior of southwestern Minnesota, often using the same locations as the Lake Benton people. They stored food in large pits dug into the ground, which meant that the villages probably were not abandoned in the winter. They buried their dead in large cemeteries, but did not construct mounds above them.

West of Mankato in the Minnesota River Valley, another village complex developed. The largest village was next to the present day town of Cambria, hence the name for the prehistoric villagers and their distinctive pottery. Cambria peoples had a lifestyle similar to Blue Earth peoples, but we have some evidence that their villages were actually fortified with stockade walls not unlike frontier forts of the U.S. Cavalry. Cambria pottery is finely made and highly decorated. It is tempered with crushed rock. Some of it resembles pottery found at the Cahokia complex near St. Louis, leading to speculation that the main Cambria village may have been a trading outpost of the Cahokians. Like Blue Earth peoples, Cambria peoples depended on corn and diverse wild food resources, but bison do not appear to have been a staple.

In the interior of southwestern Minnesota, scattered evidences for Cambria and Blue Earth campsites can be found, but only one major village has been found associated with another horticultural group dating to about one thousand years ago. Northwest of Slayton in Murray County there was a major lake complex that was drained in the early part of the 20th century. This lake complex fostered the growth of a large woods that was called the "Great Oasis" by early fur traders.

In the middle of the Great Oasis on what once was an island, archaeologists in the 1940s excavated the remains of an ancient village

which yielded a distinctive pottery type featuring fine-trailed lines on the rims of globular vessels. The pottery was called Great Oasis and it has subsequently been found at a few other island campsites in the prairie lake region. Minnesota Great Oasis sites are peripheral to the core Great Oasis development, which is in northwestern Iowa. Great Oasis sites have been found as far east as Illinois and as far west as central Nebraska. Great Oasis peoples appear to be the forebearers of the village complexes of the Missouri River trench in the Dakotas.

Great Oasis peoples in northwestern Iowa lived in large, semi-subterranean, rectangular houses in river valley villages. They grew corn and hunted bison. In Minnesota, Great Oasis sites are on islands in lakes. Storage pits are found, but there is no evidence for houses at the Minnesota sites. Corn is found, but no evidence for local cultivation. The way of life seems very similar to that of the Fox Lake and Lake Benton peoples. Some archaeologists believe that Minnesota Great Oasis is the beginning of the complex, while others believe Great Oasis sites in Minnesota are just seasonal hunting camps of people from farther south.

In western Minnesota, horticultural village peoples also lived near the headwaters of the Minnesota River. Small village sites and burial mounds on Lake Traverse and Big Stone Lake have yielded pottery that is similar to some forms of Cambria pottery, but pottery from these sites also resembles Lake Benton types. Some sites feature small fortification ditches. These ditches may be the remains of forts

that functioned much as did medieval keeps, offering temporary protection in times of danger.

This western Minnesota complex has been called Big Stone and may be the remains of the last prehistoric horticultural villagers in the prairie lake region. Big Stone peoples may be a blend of Lake Benton peoples and Cambria peoples who fled the westward march of the Oneota. Bison hunting was a big part of their lives and they supplemented it with corn and local wild foods.

People of Yesterday, People of Today

The fate of the Lake Benton peoples is unknown. Some no doubt blended with the intruders, taking up their technologies and ways of life. Some no doubt resisted change in the fastness of their island villages lost among the maze of lakes. All we can say is that there is little evidence for them after the year 1200 A.D.

Great Oasis, Cambria, and Blue Earth peoples appear to be gone by A.D. 1300. Big Stone peoples may survive in western Minnesota for several more centuries. By the time the French start exploring the Upper Midwest in the later part of the 1600s, southwestern Minnesota appears to be a contested zone with few permanent villages. Teton and Yankton Dakota are present in the north, while groups like the Oto, Ioway, and Omaha are present in the south. Archaeologists have yet to identify any major Indian villages in southwestern Minnesota dating to the time of early European intrusion.

Southwestern Minnesota became exclusively Dakota by the end of the 18th century, first home to the Teton, then the Yankton, and finally the four bands of the Santee or Eastern Dakota: the Mdewakatonwan, the Sisseton, the Wahpekute, and the Wahpeton. Although banished from Minnesota following the War of 1862, the Dakota have managed to return and survive in small communities at Upper Sioux and Lower Sioux on the Minnesota River.

For over 10,000 years, humans have lived in southwestern Minnesota. Although the land is very different today and the technology of fluted points incomparable to that of computers, the peoples of the prairie lake region share a legacy. That legacy is a knowledge that we are all immigrants. It is making a living from a land of rich soils and shallow lakes and scattered woodlands. It is surviving thunderstorms and tornadoes in the summer and blizzards and bitter cold in the winter. It is knowing the hardships of droughts and floods. It is a self-dependence based on the knowledge that the land will survive and that each new spring brings a promise that winter cannot deny.

—Scott Anfinson

REDWOOD FALLS, 1861

aron la Hontan spoke of a great river coming in from the west, which he called "La Riviere Longue"; it is indeed very long and navigable. It is eminently the river of Minnesota (for she shares the Mississippi with Wisconsin) and it is of incalculable value to her. It flows through a very fertile country, destined to be famous for its wheat; but it is a remarkably winding stream, so that Redwood is only half as far from its mouth by land as by water. There was not a straight reach a mile in length as far as we went; generally you could not see a quarter of a mile of water, and the boat was steadily turning this way or that. At the greater bends, as at the Traverse des Sioux, some of the passengers were landed, and walked across, to be taken in on the other side. Two or three times you could have thrown a stone across the neck of the isthmus, while it was from one to three miles round it.

It was a very novel kind of navigation to me. The boat was perhaps the largest that had been up so high, and the water was rather low; it had been fifteen feet higher. In making a short turn we repeatedly and designedly ran square into the steep and soft bank, taking in a cartload of earth, this being more effectual than the rudder to fetch us about again; or the deep water was so narrow and close to the shore that we were obliged to run into and break down at least fifty trees which overhung the water, when we did not cut them off; repeatedly losing a part of our outworks, though the most exposed had been taken in. I could pluck almost any plant on the bank from the boat.

We very frequently got aground, and then drew ourselves along with a windlass and a cable fastened to a tree; or we swung round in the current, and completely blocked up and blockaded the river, one end of the boat resting on each shore. And yet we would haul ourselves round again with the windlass and cable in an hour or two; though the boat was about one hundred and sixty feet long, and drew some three feet of water, often water and sand. It was one consolation to know that in such a case we were all the while damming the river, and so raising it. We once ran fairly into a concealed rock, with a shock that aroused all the passengers. We rested there, and the mate went below with a lamp, expecting to find a hole, but he did not. Snags and sawyers were so common that I forgot to mention them. The sound of the boat rumbling over one was the ordinary music. However, as long as the boiler did not burst, we knew that no serious accident was likely to happen.

Yet it was a singularly navigable river; more so than the Mississippi above the Falls of St. Anthony; and this is owing to its very crookedness. Ditch it straight, and it would not only be very swift, but would soon run out. It was from ten to fifteen rods wide near the mouth, and from eight to ten or twelve at Redwood. Though the current was swift, I did not see a "rip" on it, and only three or four rocks. For three months in the year I am told it can be navigated by small steamers about twice as far as we went, or to its source in Big Stone Lake. A former Indian agent told me that at high water it was thought that such a steamer might pass into the Red River (of the North). The last of the

little settlements on the river was New Ulm, about a hundred miles this side of Redwood. It consists wholly of Germans. We left them a hundred barrels of salt, which will be worth something more when the water is lowest, than at present. Redwood is a mere locality, scarcely an Indian village, where there is a store, and where some houses have been built for the Indians. We were now fairly on the great plains; and, looking south and after walking three miles that way, could see no tree in that horizon. The buffalo was said to be feeding within twenty-five or thirty miles. . . .

A regular council was held at Redwood with the Indians, who had come in on their ponies; and speeches were made on both sides through an interpreter, quite in the described mode; the Indians, as usual, having the advantage in point of truth and earnestness, and therefore of eloquence. The most prominent chief was named Little Crow. They were quite dissatisfied with the white man's treatment of them, and probably have reason to be so. This council was to be continued for two or three days, the payments to be made the second day; and another payment, to other bands a little higher up, on the Yellow Medicine, a tributary of the Minnesota, a few days thereafter. In the afternoon the half-naked Indians performed a dance at the request of the Governor, for our amusement and their own benefit. Then we took leave of them, and of the officials who had come to treat with them. In the dance were thirty men dancing and twelve musicians with drums, while others struck their arrows against their bows. The dancers blew some flutes, and kept good time, moving their feet or their shoulders, sometimes one, sometimes both. They wear no shirts. Five bands of Indians came in, and were feasted on an ox cut into five parts, one for each band.

—Henry David Thoreau

TOWARD THE SUNSET

Bright, clear sky over a plain so wide that the rim of the heavens cut down on it around the entire horizon. . . . Bright, clear sky, to-day, to-morrow, and for all time to come.

. . . And sun! And still more sun! It set the heavens afire every morning; it grew with the day to quivering golden light—then softened into all the shades of red and purple as evening fell. . . . Pure colour everywhere. A gust of wind, sweeping across the plain, threw into life waves of yellow and blue and green. Now and then a dead black wave would race over the scene . . . a cloud's gliding shadow . . . now and then . . .

It was late afternoon. A small caravan was pushing its way through the tall grass. The track that it left behind was like the wake of a boat except that instead of widening out astern it closed in again.

"Tish-ah!" said the grass. . . . "Tish-ah, tish-ah!" . . . Never had it said anything else—never would it say anything else. It bent resiliently under the trampling feet; it did not break, but it complained aloud every time—for nothing like this had ever happened to it before. . . . "Tish-ah, tish-ah!" it cried, and rose up in surprise to look at this rough, hard thing that had crushed it to the ground so rudely, and then moved on.

A stocky, broad-shouldered man walked at the head of the caravan. He seemed shorter than he really was, because of the tall grass around him and the broad-brimmed hat of coarse straw which he wore. A few steps behind him followed a boy of about nine years of age. The boy's blond hair was clearly marked against his brown, sunburnt neck; but the man's hair and neck were of exactly the same shade of brown. From the looks of these two, and still more from their gait, it was easy to guess that here walked father and son.

Behind them a team of oxen jogged along; the oxen were drawing a vehicle which once upon a time might have been a wagon, but which now, on account of its many and grave infirmities, ought long since to have been consigned to the scrap heap—exactly the place, in point of fact, where the man had picked it up. Over the wagon box long willow saplings had been bent, in the form of arches in a church chancel—six of them in all. On these arches, and tied down to the body on each side, were spread first of all two hand-woven blankets,

53

that might well have adorned the walls of some manor house in the olden times; on top of the blankets were thrown two sheepskin robes, with the wool side down, which were used for bed-coverings at night. The rear of the wagon was stowed full of numberless articles, all the way up to the top. A large immigrant chest at the bottom of the pile, very long and high, devoured a big share of the space; around and above it were piled household utensils, tools, implements, and all their clothing.

Hitched to this wagon and trailing behind was another vehicle, homemade and very curious-looking, so solidly and quaintly constructed that it might easily have won a place in any museum. Indeed, it appeared strong enough to stand all the jolting from the Atlantic to the Pacific. . . . It, too, was a wagon, after a fashion; at least, it had been intended for such. The wheels were made from pieces of plank fitting

wider than that of the first wagon, was also loaded full of provisions and house-hold gear, covered over with canvas and lashed down securely. Both wagons creaked and groaned loudly every time they bounced over a tussock or hove out of a hollow. . . . "Squeak, squeak!" said the one. . . . "Squeak, squeak!" answered the other. . . . The strident sound broke the silence of centuries.

A short distance behind the wagons followed a brindle cow. The caravan moved so slowly that she occasionally had time to stop and snatch a few mouthfuls, though there was never a chance for many at a time. But what little she got in this way she sorely needed. She had been jogging along all day, swinging and switching her tail, the rudder of the caravan. Soon it would be night, and then her part of the work would come—to furnish milk for the evening porridge, for all the company up ahead.

54

Across the front end of the box of the first wagon lay a rough piece of plank. On the right side of this plank sat a woman with a white kerchief over her head driving the oxen. Against her thigh rested the blond head of a little girl, who was stretched out on the plank and sleeping sweetly. Now and then the hand of the mother moved across the child's face to chase away the mosquitoes, which had begun to gather as the sun lowered. On the left side of the plank, beyond the girl, sat a boy about seven years old—a well-grown lad, his skin deeply tanned, a certain clever, watchful gleam in his eyes. With hands folded over one knee, he looked straight ahead.

This was the caravan of Per Hansa, who with his family and all his earthly possessions was moving west from Filmore County, Minnesota, to Dakota Territory. There he intended to take up land and build himself a home; he was going to do something remarkable out there which should become known far and wide. No lack of opportunity in that country, he had been told! . . . Per Hansa himself strode ahead and laid out the course; the Boy Ole, or *Olamand,* followed closely after, and explored it. Beret, the wife, drove the oxen and took care of little Anna Marie, pet-named *And-Ongen* (which means "The Duckling"), who was usually bubbling over with happiness. Hans Kristian, whose everyday name was *Store-Hans* (meaning "Big Hans," to distinguish him from his godfather, who was also named Hans, but who, of course, was three times his size), sat there on the wagon, and saw to it that everyone attended to business. . . . The cow Rosie trailed behind, swinging and switching her tail, following the caravan farther and farther yet into the endless vista of the plain.

"Tish-ah, tish-ah!" cried the grass. . . . . "Tish-ah, tish-ah!"

—Ole Rolvaag

PULLMAN CARS AND THEIR OCCUPANTS

When we awake the next morning, we find the aspect of the country quite changed. We have entered into the prairie; not the well-cultivated prairie around Chicago, but the prairie in all its immensity and naked wildness. Here the work of colonisation is only just beginning, and in the vicinity of the stations only may be seen, here and there, far away and apart, little wooden houses with clearings around them. Everywhere else the eye wanders without any object to arrest it over an immense plain, hardly varied with a mound or a hill, and covered with thick grass, reflecting singular blue tints as it undulates under the passing breeze. Water is scarce: a few hollows filled with muddy pools trailing slowly their tortuous courses towards the Missouri; in other places the water, having no outlet, forms swamps, from which constantly rise long flocks of ducks.

The impression produced is gloomy in the extreme; for, evident as it is that incalculable riches are hidden in these monotonous plains, how many years more will our agriculturists of Europe, weighed down with burdens accumulated through many centuries of civilisation, be able to continue struggling against the invasion of products from this free land? An impulse has now been given to the movement, and to arrest it is out

of the question. Good, however, will result from it, still not before fifty years hence, when the value of our lands will have been depreciated at least one half, and the half of our peasants have been forced to emigrate. And in this interval, what suffering!

We must not close our eyes to the inevitable consequences; unless a total change takes place in the system of our customs duties the struggle will be fruitless, and every year that passes away will see the ruin of one branch or another of our agricultural industry. First the corn and next the wine, for California is beginning to send its wines to Bordeaux, after having sent us the phylloxera, and then it will be the rearing of live stock. Every line of railway that opens in the Far West, opens at the same time a new wound.

It is interesting to examine the manner in which the American government favours this movement. Sometimes, as in the case of the *Union Pacific,* the great artery that first traversed the continent, it gives directly a subsidy to the company, though lately it has not proceeded in this manner.

As soon as the course of the line is settled, the zone to be run over is divided into little squares, having their base along the line a

mile in length, each called "a section." The company, by the terms of the concession, becomes the proprietor of the half of these lands, the rest remaining with the government.

During the first years especially, the only benefits the shareholders can hope to realize, arise from the sale and rise in value of these lands; the company therefore uses every means to attract immigration thither.

The settler, as he is called, generally comes to choose his land in autumn. Upon a simple declaration, they give him a run, almost gratuitous, over the line. As soon as he has made his choice he goes in quest of the company's agent. If he has no money, as it unluckily happens in most cases, they give him a credit of five or six years. The land is sold to him at the rate of from one to five dollars the acre. He must still have a house, agricultural implements, and live stock; all these are furnished to him by special establishments. These expenses, however, are relatively considerable: a house costs from 350 to 500 dollars; a milch cow, 25 to 30 dollars; a good pair of horses, 100 or 150 dollars. But in the spring, about the 15th of April, he has only to turn the turf of the prairie and throw down a few handfuls of oats, to garner, about the end of July, 25 to 40 bushels per acre. After the first year, they sow wheat, that returns from 20 to 40 bushels the acre, and this with a simple turn of the soil, without even a spadeful of manure. They showed us lands that had given as much as twenty-five successive harvests of corn by this simple treatment, without any appreciable depreciation of the soil—a black alluvial earth, in which not a stone can be seen.

To feed his cattle in winter, the new farmer may cut as much grass for hay as he thinks proper; and if he has need of a little ready-

money for his current expenses, he has only to go to his neighbours to work a while, and he will earn two dollars a day. At the end of the first year something comes in, and if his visits to the bar at the station have not been immoderate, the farm and stock should, at the end of four or five years, be entirely his own, freed from all debt.

At Tracy, where we arrived at nine in the morning, we were obliged to leave our Pullman car, which proceeded no further. The compartment in which we are now installed contains a class quite special, entirely different from that we had been accustomed to see in the East. Four or five women of very mysterious bearing occupy one corner; they seem to be under the surveillance of a stern-looking couple. The other places are occupied by men bespattered with mud up to their ears, habited in well-worn flannel shirts, and with their breeches tucked in great long boots. They are all inveterate tobacco-chewers. There are a few women and some groups of children. At every station men with their hands full of prospectuses rush into the carriages: they are land

agents, and come up to us offering farms. One of these pushing men of business is pestering me to buy a whole quarter of a town with some sounding name, Athens or Paris, I forget which. He spreads out before me the plan. I see there grand avenues intersected by innumerable streets, and the whole well sprinkled with squares, two public gardens, seven or eight railway stations, churches and chapels by the dozen, and ten or twelve banks. When he is quite convinced I am not going to buy anything of him, he admits, pleasantly enough, that there are only one hundred and fifty inhabitants in this city, who are dwelling in about fifty wooden sheds; but he asserts that in two years there will be more than twenty thousand, and this is not at all impossible. The children begin frolicking at once, and make their *debut* by shooting adriotly a ball into the eye of the gentleman, the vendor of the city, who smiles graciously, for it is well understood that in America all the children are charming. After this comes my turn, and I immediately open the window behind me, hoping that the ball will consequently roll into the prairie. The wickedness of my proceeding is instantly detected, and the young gentleman, a terrible seven-year-old urchin, springs forward to close it with-out my permission. I oppose, and away he goes, rapping out an oath with a *resonance* that seemed to gratify his vengeance.

Every moment some one in passing along the passage reserved through the middle of the carriage, stumbles and jostles against us: they tread on our toes also, and without a word of apology. But for all that they are in one respect superior to the ill-bred class among us, inasmuch as they consider it quite natural that others should treat them in the same mode. One of my friends was travelling lately in a saloon car; all at once he was startled at seeing two great feet stretched out on each side of his face! But his neighbour behind him was merely putting himself at his ease. To have shown any indignation, of course, would not have been *comme il faut* from a Yankee point of view, and besides

60

useless. Fortunately he finds an easy chair unoccupied behind this amiable Yankee, takes possession of it, and returns the compliment precisely in the same way. The other kept as still as a mouse with the most perfect composure.

Here is another incident of the same kind that was related to me. Two travellers, the one French and the other American, were sitting face to face in a tramway. The American, who was chewing tobacco as usual, began spitting, with remarkable dexterity too, through the open window beside the Frenchman. The latter, feeling annoyed and getting irritated, would have his revenge, but sets about it so unskillfully that he hits his antagonist plain in the face. Naturally, he was overwhelmed with confusion and apologies, which were received by the Yankee with very good grace, who calmly took his handkerchief and applied it as if he were wiping away a drop of rain, remarking at the same time with a somewhat patronising tone, "All right, stranger! I guess you are a beginner!"

These people are very coarse, because they have never been taught to be otherwise; but for all that, they are in many respects superior in behaviour to people of the same class in France. Their attitude towards women is admirable. Not an obscene word in their presence ever escapes their lips. Moreover, equality with them is so thoroughly ingrafted in their minds, that one never sees, as in France, that sullen hostility so often manifested by the man in blouse towards the man in frock coat. This observation, however, though quite true with respect to the West, would at least be subject to some reservation regarding the states of the East, which are becoming rapidly Europeanised.

Around the stations are already grouped a few houses and each of these sends forth its contingent of sickly-looking ragamuffins who come, dabbling through the mud with their naked feet, to look at the train. The population of these villages is throughout of the same character. Two or three grocers, a few dry-goods stores, shoeing smiths, saddlers, one or two little chapels which do not look as if they were frequented, and hardly ever any butchers or bakers. In America they eat nothing but bacon. As for bread, everyone makes at home for each meal balls of a sort of unfermented paste, baked in a stove, as a substitute! Accordingly, especially in the West, nine Americans out of ten who have reached the age of twenty are afflicted with chronic gastritis.

But there are some things never wanting—an hotel for instance, and then a collection of "saloons." It is under this fine name that the public houses and taverns are known, and it is here where the best part of the profits of the farms around changes hands. Before the doors endless files of agricultural machines, thrashers, harvesters, mowers, all painted in bright colours, are displayed. Their employment, which with us in France is only yet exceptional, is quite the rule here. The well-

levelled soil of the prairie, besides, seems specially adapted to their use.

As we proceed on our way the number of our travelling companions diminishes in the same ratio. At one of the last stations two *cow-boys* get into the train. With their bossy felt hats set off with tarnished gold lace, their great boots bristling with Mexican spurs, and their girdles furnished with a brace of Colts' revolvers, cartridges, and a murderous, big knife, these "boys" have the look of actual bandits. These in our company behave very well, but it is not always so with these gentry. A few weeks ago a drunken cow-boy, intent on indulging, it seems, in one of their favourite pastimes, shot away the cigar from an inoffensive neighbour with a ball from his revolver. Thereupon the guard blew out his brains with his pistol on the spot; the body was cast out on the line, and everything thus promptly settled without bier, bell, or burial.

These cow-boys are the plague of the West. Recruited generally from among men too idle to work in the mines or on the farms, passing their life on the prairie, day and night in the saddle, watching their herds, constantly at war with the Indians, they make their appearance in the towns only on pay days, when they invariably get drunk and become a terror to the inhabitants, who, on the other hand, get as much profit out of them as they can, regarding them as very proper subjects for *exploitation.* The newspapers, romances,

and tales are full of their exploits. Now and then one hears that a troop of cow-boys have taken possession of a little town on the frontier and pillaged the inhabitants, or that, solely from mere wantonness and wild spirits, they had driven all the population to a certain spot, and there forced them to dance for hours together before them for their diversion, sending bullets into the calves of their legs if the performance did not proceed with sufficient animation. Then some fine day a Vigilance Committee is formed, who take three or four unlucky individuals by mere chance, and hang them at the first tree they come to, the others continuing their exploits a little further off.

After all, they are the best boys in the world in the estimation of the saloon keepers, whose fortunes they make.

—Baron E. de Mandat-Grace

Cottonwoods

In the cottonwood grove
behind Dahl's farm
the eyes of rusting cars
stare at me before
I crawl into them,
pretend I am driving;
power flows from the wheels,

I believe I am in control,
forget my mother's heart
lies fading in the little bedroom
beyond the rows of corn.

They have sent me away
from her dying to play in the grove,
to sit in old cars,
to whisper into the ears of corn,
towering above me as I sit between the rows
reading her letters
which say she misses me,
even though it is quieter without me
and my brother fighting.
He has brought her a goldfish
from the little pond
beside the pergola house
and laid it on her stomach.

Years later I return to the grove,
where the cottonwood trees
have grown scrawny,
but the old cars are still there,
their eyes stare at me,
unseeing and dead.

—Phebe Hanson

In an Icelandic Graveyard

A woman and I are in an old Icelandic graveyard on a windy treeless hill in western Minnesota. She has never been here. She sees her own name on every tombstone. Sometimes she died an old lady, surrounded by children and grandchildren and great-grandchildren, like the petals around the center of a flower. Sometimes she died as a child who could barely speak—without the water of God on his hairless head. Sometimes her name is spelled right, and sometimes not. It is a good thing to have died so many times, to feel so often the death shudder in the bones—so that now the muscles are practiced at it—and it can be done with the graceful, delicate movements of a dancer.

—Bill Holm

The Grandfathers

Gudmundsson, Olson, Peturson, Josefson,
Williamson, Anderson, Olafson, Hallgrimson.

In these graves sleep the founders of the kingdom,
below the dying elms, their branches bowed
like the vaults of Trondheim Cathedral.

Hanson, Benson, Sigurdson, Peterson,
Björnson, Rafnsson, Jonason, Arngrimson.

In the cycles of seasons their lives unwound,
in fields of ripening corn and wheat,
in the white wilderness of prairie winter.

Nicholson, Erickson, Högnason, Johnson,
Thordarson, Thorsteinson, Magnusson, Guttormsson.

Far beyond the western rim of South Dakota
the sun sets over the grave of Johann Kristjan Johannson.
He dreams dreams unbroken as the snow-covered prairie.

—David Pichaske

ETHNICITY AND SETTLEMENT IN SOUTHWESTERN MINNESOTA

On June 20, 1886, Anna Felcyn, age 29, the wife of Michal Felcyn and the mother of three young children and stepmother to several more, died after a long illness in a sod hut near Wilno in Lincoln County. Two days after her death, the entire Polish community of the Wilno area turned out for her funeral. At 8 o'clock on the morning of June 22nd, accompanied by a procession of over thirty wagons filled with mourners, her body was taken from the home. For the next six hours the procession visited nearly every Polish home in the area, some located miles apart, finally ending up at the Church of St. John Cantius in Wilno where the funeral Mass was held. After the Mass, the procession reassembled for the half-mile trip to the cemetery. At the graveside, the Poles held another service, featuring a lengthy sermon delivered by Fr. Henryk Jazdzewski. So powerful were the young priest's words that, as one eyewitness put it, "everyone present . . . was moved to tears."

Like many of the ethnic groups that settled southwestern Minnesota in the decades following the end of Civil War, the Poles of Lincoln County lived a life apart. Few of the events they considered important were ever reported by the local English-language newspapers, and few of the things the local papers ran concerning the Poles appeared in the reports they sent to Polish newspapers in Winona or Chicago. Most of the reports the Poles considered important related to their religious and cultural life. Most the early reports in the English-language papers concerned the Poles' seemly alien behavior and their alleged propensity for drunkenness and criminality. Were it not for the occasional reports the Lincoln County Poles sent to Polish-language newspapers, their rich community life—unknown even to most of their descendants—would have gone to the grave along with those early immigrant pioneers. Today, those reports, many little more than a century old, seem like messages from a lost world.

Although Poles may have been among the more "alien" groups to settle southwest Minnesota, they were not unique in having been ignored in the contemporary English-language press and largely overlooked by later observers. Settlement of southwestern Minnesota took place as a series of separate but related events that resulted in a web of parallel but isolated ethnic settlements, usually in rural areas, held together by rail lines and a series of towns that were often ethnically mixed but usually dominated by a Yankee business class.

Just as the railroad companies played a major role in creating the region's economic geography, so, too, did they shape its ethnic landscape. Railroads had clear ideas of which groups were best suited to certain tasks. Yankees and immigrants from the British Isles were usually preferred as merchants. Germans, Belgians, Dutch, French Canadians, Poles, and Czechs were seen as suitable farmers to populate the countryside. Scandinavians were also encouraged to go into farming, although the railroads were not adverse to Scandinavian or German artisans or small businessmen.

There were always exceptions to this rule. In Tyler, for example, the economic crisis of the early 1890s drove out many Yankee

businessmen just as a new wave of Danes began arriving in the area. The Danish newcomers quickly bought out the Yankees and set up their own businesses. In Ivanhoe, established by the railroad in 1900, the well-established Polish farming community in surrounding townships was able to secure a foothold in the business community despite an influx of Yankees and other groups associated with the railroad.

Except in towns like Tyler, ethnic groups that arrived after the founding of nearby railroad towns made

slow inroads into the local business and leadership class. Marshall and the surrounding area were settled by Yankees, including quite a few Civil War veterans. Although Yankee farmers soon gave way to Belgian, French Canadian, and German farmers, Yankees remained dominant in the city itself. Although French Canadians and Germans made some inroads after World War I, Belgians did not begin to move into the city until sometime after 1950. The few Belgians or French Canadians found in Marshall prior to World War I tended to be laborers. Most domestic servants in Marshall were young women of foreign parentage, Icelanders, Norwegians, or Poles whose families resided outside the city in most cases.

Whereas the railroad towns of the region proved relatively resistant to ethnic change in the first few generations of settlement, the countryside proved to be another matter. The earlier Yankee, British Canadian, English, Welsh, and, in some cases, Irish settlers, tended to sell their farms to new groups and provide their children with more education rather than a place on the land. Their place was usually taken by Germans, Belgians, or Poles. In 1885 the *Lake Benton News* reported that "Mr. Alexander

of Royal [Township] has sold to Polanders and gone south. This township will soon be exclusively occupied by Polanders."

Other ethnic groups, such as Norwegians, Swedes, and French Canadians settled as farmers and followed the path of the Yankees, albeit one generation later. At one point prior to 1920 it was believed that Marshall would become an important French-Canadian center. The French Canadians did come in significant numbers, but by World War II they were moving out. In Lyon County the net effect of this, over time, was to concentrate Belgians on the land to the point where they became the dominant rural group in the county.

Many of the area's smaller groups have had an equally transient history. After the turn of the twentieth century, Marshall began to

attract a small community of east European Jews. Most were small businessmen, although one Jewish businessman parleyed a junk-buying business into a multi-million dollar food-processing empire. Most Jewish families saw themselves as separate from the larger community, but despite isolated incidents of anti-Semitism they adapted well to the small-town environment. One Jewish businessman was even elected mayor. By the 1970s and 1980s, however, most of Marshall's Jewish families had moved on as educational and business opportunities beckoned elsewhere.

Mexicans have been particularly mobile. Since before World War I small groups moved in and out of the area. Some came to work in small, local factories, but the majority were migrant farm laborers. Beginning in the 1970s, towns like Marshall and Willmar acquired more permanent Mexican and Mexican-American residents, with large numbers arriving in the early 1990s to work in the region's poultry processing plants. Vietnamese, who came to the U.S. as the result of political upheavals in their homeland in the 1970s, were resettled in many of the area's towns but soon moved to larger Vietnamese enclaves in the Twin Cities or on the West Coast.

The process of creating ethnic enclaves in town and countryside was furthered by ethnic colonization schemes conducted in cooperation with the railroad. Danish settlement around Tyler, Polish settlement around Wilno/Ivanhoe, and the initial Belgian settlement around Ghent were planned by promoters, churches, and the railroads. These efforts usually attracted a large group of initial settlers followed by a steady influx of acquaintances, friends, and relatives over the next several years. Even when the process was slower and less dramatic, the process of settlement tended to create distinct ethnic enclaves in the countryside.

In some cases this process was furthered by the creation of inland towns (towns not established by the railroad and without rail service).

Wilno for the Poles of Lincoln County and Bechyn for the Czechs of Renville County provided distinct niches with their own institutions: a church, a saloon, a general store, and, usually, a blacksmith, all owned and operated by fellow countrymen. Only in the case of the Germans in New Ulm was an ethnic group able to dominate a larger town, and in that case such ethnic dominance became a public target during the patriotic excesses of World War I.

In many ways the ethnic settlements in rural southwest Minnesota resembled spread-out versions of ethnic neighborhoods in large cities. In describing many of the Icelanders he knew in Minnesota, writer Bill Holm has aptly noted that many seemed as if they did not

quite live in America. Indeed, most had one foot in America and one foot in their ancestral homelands. Even their language patterns mirrored this split. In post-World War II Ivanhoe, one observer noted, second- and third-generation Polish immigrants often spoke a mixture of Polish and English, starting a sentence in one language and finishing it in another.

Most ethnic farmers and businesspeople were fully assimilated economically. They carried on economic relationships freely with their neighbors of other ethnic and religious backgrounds, using English as a common language. Yet most groups remained separate culturally at least into the 1960s when increasing levels of education began breaking down the barriers. Until that time, people in the countryside tended to choose marriage partners from within their own religious/ethnic group.

Time has blurred the ethnic enclaves of the settlement era in southwestern Minnesota, but their effect on the lives and minds of the region's population are still quite manifest. Voting patterns for ethnic townships have remained remarkably consistent over time.

The creation of ethnic festivals such as Belgian-American Days (Ghent), Polska Kielbasa Days (Ivanhoe), or Abelskiver Days (Tyler) show that ethnic identity has taken on new functions in the lives of the region's people. It indicates that their ethnicity has become "safe" and non-threatening. On more than one occasion local residents have under-emphasized the chilly welcome their own forebearers received and overestimated the speed at which those forebearers came to fit comfortably into American society. This historical revision

has been prompted, in part, by the arrival of newcomers, such as Mexicans who, like the Poles or Belgians of an earlier era, are seen as threatening and impossible to assimilate.

Although buried by time and hidden underneath a veneer of mass culture, ethnicity remains an important facet of life in southwestern Minnesota. Its impact on the region's past (and consequently its present) is profound and abiding. As new ethnic groups continue to arrive on their own historical trajectories, ethnicity and the feelings it evokes will continue to be a shaping influence on the region and its people.

—John Radzilowski

THE LAND OF THE STRADDLE-BUG

Like other pre-emptors I was forced to hold my claim by visiting it once every thirty days, and these trips became each time more painful, more menacing. February and March were of pitiless severity. One blizzard followed another with ever-increasing fury. No sooner was the snow laid by a north wind than it took wing above a southern blast and returned upon us sifting to and fro until at last its crystals were as fine as flour, so triturated that it seemed to drive through an inch board. Often it filled the air for hundreds of feet above the earth like a mist, and lay in long ridges behind every bush or weed. Nothing lived on these desolate uplands but the white owl and the wolf.

One cold, bright day I started for my claim accompanied by a young Englishman, a fair faced delicate young clerk from London, and before we had covered half our journey the west wind met us with such fury that the little cockney would certainly have frozen had I not forced him out of the sleigh to run by its side.

Poor little man! This was not the romantic home he had expected to gain when he left his office on the Strand. Luckily, his wretched shanty was some six miles nearer than mine or he would have died. Leaving him safe in his den, I pushed on toward my own claim, in the teeth of a terrific gale, the cold growing each moment more intense. "The sunset regions" at that moment did not provoke me to song.

In order to reach my cabin before darkness fell, I urged my team desperately, and it was well that I did, for I could scarcely see my horses during the last mile, and the wind was appalling even to me—an experienced plainsman. Arriving at the barn I was disheartened to find the doors heavily banked with snow, but I fell to in desperate haste, and soon shoveled a passageway.

This warmed me, but in the delay one of my horses became so chilled that he could scarcely enter his stall. He refused to eat also, and this troubled me very much. However, I loaded him with blankets and fell to work rubbing his legs with wisps of hay, to start the circulation, and did not desist until the old fellow began nibbling his forage.

By this time the wind was blowing seventy miles an hour, and black darkness was upon the land. With a rush I reached my shanty only to find that somebody had taken all my coal and nearly all my kindling, save a few pieces of pine. This was serious, but I kindled a fire with the blocks, a blaze which was especially grateful by reason of its quick response.

Hardly was the stove in action, when a rap at the door startled me. "Come," I shouted. In answer to my call, a young man, a neighbor, entered, carrying a sack filled with coal. He explained with some embarrassment, that in his extremity during the preceding blizzard, he had borrowed from my store, and that (upon seeing my light) he had hurried to restore the fuel, enough, at any rate, to last out the night. His

heroism appeased my wrath and I watched him setting out on his return journey with genuine anxiety.

That night is still vivid in my memory. The frail shanty, cowering close, quivered in the wind like a frightened hare. The powdery snow appeared to drive directly through the solid boards, and each hour the mercury slowly sank. Drawing my bed close to the fire, I covered myself with a buffalo robe and so slept for an hour or two.

When I woke it was still dark and the wind, though terrifying, was intermittent in its attack. The timbers of the house creaked as the blast lay hard upon it, and now and again the faint fine crystals came sifting down upon my face—driven beneath the shingles by the tempest. At last I lit my oil lamp and shivered in my robe till dawn.

The morning came, bright with sun but with the thermometer forty degrees below zero. It was so cold that the horses refused to face the northwest wind. I could not hitch them to the sleigh until I had blanketed them both beneath their harness; even then they snorted and pawed in terror. At last, having succeeded in hooking the traces I sprang in and, wrapping the robe about me, pushed eastward with all speed, seeking food and fire.

This may be taken as a turning point in my career, for this experience (followed by two others almost as severe) permanently chilled my enthusiasm for pioneering the plain. Never again did I sing "Sunset Regions" with the same exultant spirit. "O'er the hills in legions, boys," no longer meant sunlit savannahs, flower meadows and deer-filled glades. The mingled "wood and prairie land" of the song was gone and Uncle Sam's domain, bleak, semi-arid, and wind-swept, offered little charm to my imagination. From that little cabin on the ridge I turned my face toward settlement, eager to escape the terror and the loneliness of the treeless sod. I began to plan for other work in other airs.

—Hamlin Garland

Reflections in Sleepy Eye

For Robert Bly

3,489 friendly people
Elm grove, willow, Blue Earth County's
    red barns, tiny feoff with
    gas nozzle snout on hillock,
Large beetles & lizards—
    orange-painted steel
    cranes & truck cabs,
    Green seeder down-pointed
      Science Toy earth-cock.
Thin floods, smooth planted acres
    upturned, brown
    cornstubble plowed under,
    tractor pulling discs over fenced land.
Old box-alder fallen over
    on knees in pond-flood,
white painted gas tanks by
    Springfield's rail yard woods,
    tiny train parade by Meats
    Groceries North Star Seeds
Our Flag at full mast
    TV antennae, large leafy antennaed
    trees upstretched green,
    Sheep on stormfenced knoll,
    green little wood acres—
one forest from Canada to these
plains—Corn silage in net bins,
    Windmills in Tracy,
    Blue enamel silos cap'd
    aluminum, minarets in white sunbeam.
Cannabis excellent for drying lymph-
    glands, specific relief for
    symptoms of colds, flu,
    ear pressure grippe &
Eustachian tube clogging—

A tree, bent broken mid-trunk
    branches to ground—
Much land, few folk, excelsior grave
    yard stones
    silver tipp'd phalloi to heaven—
Aum, Om, Ford, Mailbox
    telephone pole wire strung
    down road. Lake house
    fence poles, tree shade
    pine hill grave, Ah
Lake Benton's blue waved waters—
    finally, Time came to
    the brick barn! collapsed!
Old oak trunk sunk thick
    under ground.
Farm car ploughman rolling discs,
    iron cuts smooth ground even,
    hill plains roll—
Cows browse under alder shoot,
    bent limbs arch clear brown
    stream beds, trees stand
    on banks observing
shade, peculiar standing up or kneeling
    groundward
Car graveyard fills eyes
    iron glitters, chrome fenders
    rust—
White crosses, Vietnam War Dead
    churchbells ring
Cars, kids, hamburger stand
    open, barn-smile
    white eye, door mouth.

—Allen Ginsberg

78

HOME

The town of Lake Wobegon, Minnesota, lies on the shore against Adams Hill, looking east across the blue-green water to the dark woods. From the south, the highway aims for the lake, bends hard left by the magnificent concrete Grecian grain silo, and eases over a leg of the hill past the SLOW CHILDREN sign, bringing the traveler in on Main Street toward the town's one traffic light, which is almost always green. A few surviving elms shade the street. Along the ragged dirt path between the asphalt and the grass, a child slowly walks to Ralph's Grocery, kicking an asphalt chunk ahead of him. It is a chunk that after four blocks he is now mesmerized by, to which he is completely dedicated. At Bunsen Motors, the sidewalk begins. A breeze off the lake brings in a sweet air of mud and rotting wood, a slight fishy smell, and picks up the sweetness of old grease, a sharp whiff of gasoline, fresh tires, spring dust, and, from across the street, the faint essence of tuna hotdish at the Chatterbox Cafe. A stout figure in green coveralls disappears inside. The boy kicks the chunk at the curb, once, twice, then lofts it over the curb and sidewalk across the concrete to the island of Pure Oil pumps. He jumps three times on the Bunsen bell hose, making three dings back in the dark garage. The mayor of Lake Wobegon, Clint Bunsen, peers out from the grease pit, under a black Ford pickup. His brother Clarence, wiping the showroom glass (BUNSEN MOTORS — FORD — NEW & USED — SALES & SERVICE) with an old blue shirt, knocks on the window. The showroom is empty. The boy follows the chunk north a few doors to Ralph's window, which displays a mournful cardboard pig, his body marked with the names of cuts. An old man sits on Ralph's bench, white hair as fine as spun glass poking out under his green feed cap, his grizzled chin on his skinny chest, snoozing, the afternoon sun now reaching under the faded brown canvas awning up to his belt. He is not Ralph. Ralph is the thin man in the white apron who has stepped out the back door of the store, away from the meat counter, to get a breath of fresh, meatless air. He stands on a rickety porch that looks across the lake, a stone's throw away. The beach there is stony; the sandy beach is two blocks to the north. A girl, perhaps one of his, stands on the diving dock, plugs her nose, and executes a perfect cannonball, and he hears the dull *thunsh*. A quarter-mile away, a silver boat sits off the weeds in Sunfish Bay; a man in a bright blue jacket waves his pole; the line is hooked on weeds. The sun makes a trail of shimmering lights across the water. It would make quite a picture if you had the right lens, which nobody in this town has got.

—Garrison Keillor

How to Take a Walk

This is farming country.
The neighbors will believe
you are crazy
if you take a walk
just to think and be alone.
So carry a shotgun
and walk the fence line.
Pretend you are hunting
and your walking will not
arouse suspicion.
But don't forget
to load the shotgun.
They will know
if your gun is empty.
Stop occasionally.
Cock your head and listen
to the doves you never see.
Part the tall weeds
with your hand and inspect
the ground.

Sniff the air as a hunter would.
(That wonderful smell
of sweet clover is a bonus.)
Soon you will forget
the gun in your hands,
but remember, someone
may be watching.
If you hear beating wings
and see the bronze flash
of something flying up,
you will have to shoot it.

—Leo Dangel

MY FATHER

My first memory of my father was the day he caught a ride to town with a neighbor and later in the afternoon, to our surprise, came rolling onto the yard driving a new car, a chain-drive Overland, beeping the bulb horn, scaring the dog into hiding under the corncrib, making the cattle bawl out in the barnyard, causing the horses out in the night yard to pop their tails, and chasing the chickens back into their coops. My mother appeared at the screen door to the kitchen, drying her hands in her green apron and wondering what all the racket was about. My father invited her to get in and he'd take us all for a spin around the section. My brother Edward and I quickly climbed in back, our usual seat in the carriage, breaths short for joy, eyes as wild as cock-eyed roosters. My mother got in very reluctantly. She didn't like "the automobile" as she always called it. Pa bugled the horn again and we were off. The sun was shining and all the neighbors' chickens were working the ditches for grasshoppers. When Pa blew the horn, the chickens sprayed in all directions. The front of the Overland went through them like the prow of a boat pushing through white water. When the ride was over, my mother got out of the car, not saying a word, and with a sick smile went directly back to her kitchen. Ma never did get to like "the automobile" and so long as she was alive she never permitted Pa to drive over 30 miles an hour. "Or I jump out."

Pa continued to surprise us when he came back from trips. One day he went to Sioux City with a shipment of hogs, taking the Great Northern from Doon. A day later he arrived home catching a ride with a neighbor. Eddie and I ran out to the gate to see who it was. When Pa stepped out of the car we didn't recognize him right away. Pa had bought himself a complete set of new clothes, a new gray overcoat with a black velvet collar, a new gray hat with a black band, a new gray suit, and a pair of black gloves. The face looked familiar but all those new

85

clothes threw us off. Also this strange man with Pa's face didn't act like Pa. This man acted like a high monkey-monk from the city with fancy dude manners. He had a package with him which he carried into the kitchen and proceeded to open. It turned out to be a special dress, floor length, for my mother. It was when Pa took off his hat and bowed to Ma and kissed her that I finally made out for sure who it really was.

One day I heard some coughing in the barn and when I looked I found Pa's favorite horse Daise down. I'd known he'd kept her in the barn that day for some reason, but I was shocked to see Daise lying on the floor. One never caught a horse down. I ran to get my father in the house. Pa was smoking his pipe, feet up on the reservoir of the stove. When I told him what I'd seen, Pa clapped out his pipe in the range, and hurried out to the barn. Pa took one look and knew the worst. He got down on his knees beside her and held her head.

After a while Daise coughed in his lap. That ignited Pa. He gently laid her head down in the straw and ran to the house to call the veterinarian. When my mother wondered a little about the cost of the long distance call, my father whirled on her and cried, "My God, woman, that's Daise that's sick! My Daise! You know, the pretty roan what's been with me all these years. Who even took me to Orange City to see you."

When he couldn't raise the vet, Pa asked Ma if she had some liniment around. She didn't. So next he asked her for the whiskey bottle lying in the bottom of her wardrobe. She gave it to him reluctantly. He ran to the barn with the whiskey to give Daise a slug of it. But Daise only coughed when he opened her lips and poured some into her mouth. The whiskey spilled out into the straw.

Daise was dead within the hour.

My father cried.

I'd never before seen him cry and I was too petrified to move. I didn't want to see it but at the same time I couldn't move either. Pa dug a huge hole for Daise in the pasture and buried her. He refused to call the rendering plant.

I was about nine when my father awakened me in the middle of the night one March. He was full of tender concern, which surprised

me. What was up? I soon learned. After I'd dressed we went to the hog barn. There he explained to me what he wanted. He had purebred Poland China sows, with papers, and they had one fault. Because of special breeding they often had difficulty giving birth. What was needed was a long slim arm to reach inside the sow to help the little piglets down the birth canal. Somewhat numb, and curiously also liking what I was doing, I helped most of those sows have their pigs that spring.

Later that year hog cholera hit. The vet came too late to give the little pigs serum and they all died. My father once again cried, and then retired to his favorite spot beside the kitchen stove, feet up on the reservoir, pipe clamped tight in his mouth. He refused to move. Ma didn't know what to do with him. Finally I took it upon myself to get out the old walking plow and open up a long deep furrow in the hog pasture and bury all the little pigs. They'd begun to stink and were covered with green flies. Gone was Pa's dream that by selling purebred hogs he could finally make a killing and then buy himself a farm. He and mother dreamed every spring that someday they'd own a farm and be independent. Both hated being renters. Pa with his brother Nick and his three sisters Kathryn and Jennie and Gertrude owned Grampa Feikema's cement block house in town, but that was not the same thing as owning a real farm.

It was about the same time that an investment man heard that Pa and Ma had managed over the years to build up a savings account of some fifteen hundred dollars. The man persuaded them to invest half of it, seven hundred fifty dollars, in the Northwest Harness Company. It happened that Pa liked the Northwest harness for farm work. Pa thought them the sure thing. The man told Pa and Ma they were bound to double, if not triple, their money in a year's time. The company was new and was sure to grow. With fifteen hundred, possibly even two thousand two hundred fifty dollars, they would finally have enough to buy the farm they had their eye on. It would help make up for the loss of all those purebred Poland China pigs. But in 1922, during a recession, the Northwest Harness Company filed for bankruptcy.

That same summer Pa and Ma invested the remaining seven hundred fifty dollars in their savings account in a general store that a friend of theirs built in Lakewood, halfway between Doon and Rock Rapids, Iowa, for the convenience of nearby farmers. On stormy days, rain or snow, both Doon and Rock Rapids were pretty far away for quick shopping. Lakewood, unincorporated, had a grain elevator, a depot, a lumberyard, and a blacksmith. There were five houses.

One afternoon, no one knows how, a fire started in the storekeeper's house and then jumped across to the general store. There was no fire-fighting equipment in town. Ma learned about it via the country telephone when Central gave the alarm with a general ring. Pa with the whole family drove like mad to the final hill. When he saw how far along the fire was, he pulled up. Pa and Ma watched it all burn down from the hilltop. I remember staring down at the two great pillars of flames and smoke with a boy's deep sick feeling in my stomach. There went another seven hundred fifty dollars.

When there was nothing but ashes left, Pa turned the car around and drove home. All he said was, "Couldn't even get close enough to light my pipe with it."

—Frederick Manfred

Autumn Waiting

Cold wind.
The day is waiting for winter
Without a sound.
Everything is waiting—
Broken-down cars in the dead weeds.
The weeds themselves.
Trees.
Even sunlight
Is in no hurry and stays
For a long time
On each cornstalk.
Blackbirds are silent
And sit in piles.
From a distance
They look like
Something
Spilled on the road.

—Tom Hennen

LEARNING TO SWIM

There was Beverly, hacking her way through the water as if she were cutting a path, clearing the way to the raft. Here was I, dabbling with my toes. There was she, *diving*. Well, belly flopping, but it was advanced belly flopping, with a purposeful, unabashed flair to it. Each time she hoisted herself onto the raft with her chow-mein-noodle arms, she'd hitch up her cotton underpants with the pink rosebuds on them, and then fling herself fearlessly back into the deep, dark ice water.

I poked along back to the shore and stood on the sand, where a delicate, brackish foam, like a lace frill, gathered at the water's edge. Slowly, pulling my courage together, I inched forward, encouraging myself by reporting silently, "Now it's covering your feet. Now it's over the little white scar where you got cut on a nail in Aunt Betty's garage. Now it's at the bottom of your knees." After a long time it reached my waist, and I ducked under to let the water cover my shoulders. It was colder than the inside of our refrigerator.

A hundred or more children and grown-ups were splashing and swimming and playing games. I tried to find an empty space to practice the dead man's float. Now and then a vacant five feet or so would appear, and I'd lay myself out on it, bobbing like a cork until I ran out of breath or someone knocked into me. I loved the quality of sound when my ears were covered by water, the shouts and jokes and merry-go-round music muffled to murmurs, like those coaxing voices that drift into your ears from far away when you are falling asleep.

Then Beverly was there, pushing my head down further. I came up splattering and coughing. "Don't do that!"

Hands on her hips, bony chicken breast thrust out, she laughed and promised, "I'll teach you how to swim."

"Really?"

"Sure. You know how to float. I seen you floating."

I nodded.

"Well, watch me." She lay down on the water, arms extended ahead of her, floating as I had. Then she began to kick. Shlupp, shlupp, shlupp. And she was moving forward a little. I was amazed and delighted. That was something *I* could do. When Beverly stood up,

I lay out and kicked my feet. Sure enough, I moved a little, too.

When I planted my feet to rest and breathe, Beverly ordered, "Now watch this." Again she lay down in the dead man's float. After a moment she began to kick. When she had propelled herself a short distance, her arms, one after the other, rose out of the water and flailed down through it, to reemerge a second later and repeat the arc. It was hardly graceful, but there was no denying that Beverly advanced through the little jostling waves.

"You see," she said, returning to where I stood, "swimming is just like the dead man's float with kicking and hitting."

She was absolutely right. Why hadn't I seen that? I lay down as she had, began to kick as before, and when I'd got that rhythm going, I started slapping away at the water as if I had carpet beaters attached to my shoulders. It took so long to coordinate all of this that I was nearly out of breath before I got organized, but I was going forward, even against the waves, and excitement overtook me so strongly I forgot to hold my breath. Choking, I waded back to shallow water, for I had plowed out into depths nearly over my head. I threw my arms around Beverly. "Thank you."

"Godsakes," she muttered, backing away.

"I can swim."

"There's more to it," she pointed out practically. "You don't know how to breathe." Once more she admonished me to watch, though she needn't have bothered. Nothing could have induced me to look away. Beverly was sharing her *power*, and I was deeply impressed by her generosity.

As I watched, she repeated her previous lessons, but this time when she'd whipped along for several feet, she lifted her head straight out of the water and gulped air. Then she resumed whipping and kicking. This was the tricky part, keeping yourself afloat while you raised your head to breathe.

I gave it a try, raising my head, glimpsing a rushing world of water and light, drinking half a glass of lake water as the swells from my own efforts sloshed into my open mouth. Sputtering and spitting, I waded sheepishly back to Beverly.

"I did that when I was learning," she said.

"So did Charlie."

Charlie? Charlie was her little brother, a year younger than Beverly and me. Charlie was only in kindergarten. "Charlie can swim?"

"Sure." She waited for me to get my breath. "Try again," she exhorted.

Again and again I tried, each time taking on water until I began to feel half drowned. Still I was buoyed by accomplishment. I was swimming, sometimes only a couple of yards, but *swimming*. This was one of the best days of my life. Life could go by, weeks and months of it, and you didn't feel that you were growing any older or any bigger. Then unexpectedly a day would come along when you learned something valuable, something powerful, and afterward you were bigger and older, and you knew it. And forever you loved the person who had taught you.

—Faith Sullivan

WHAT HAPPENED DURING THE ICE STORM

One winter there was a freezing rain. How beautiful! people said when things outside started to shine with ice. But the freezing rain kept coming. Tree branches glistened like glass. Then broke like glass. Ice thickened on the windows until everything outside blurred. Farmers moved their livestock into the barns, and most animals were safe. But not the pheasants. Their eyes froze shut.

Some farmers went ice-skating down the gravel roads with clubs to harvest pheasants that sat helplessly in the roadside ditches. The boys went out into the freezing rain to find pheasants too. They saw dark spots along a fence. Pheasants, all right. Five or six of them. The boys slid their feet along slowly, trying not to break the ice that covered the snow. They slid up close to the pheasants. The pheasants pulled their heads down between their wings. They couldn't tell how easy it was to see them huddled there.

The boys stood still in the icy rain. Their breath came out in slow puffs of steam. The pheasants' breath came out in quick little white puffs. One lifted its head and turned it from side to side, but the pheasant was blind-folded with ice and didn't flush.

The boys had not brought clubs, or sacks, or anything but themselves. They stood over the pheasants, turning their own heads, looking at each other, each expecting the other to do something. To pounce on a pheasant, or to yell Bang! Things around them were shining and dripping with icy rain. The barbed-wire fence. The fence posts. The broken stems of grass. Even the grass seeds. The grass seeds looked like little yolks inside gelatin whites. And the pheasants looked like unborn birds glazed in egg white. Ice was hardening on the boys' caps and coats. Soon they would be covered with ice too.

Then one of the boys said, Shh. He was taking off his coat, the thin layer of ice splintering in flakes as he pulled his arms from the sleeves. But the inside of the coat was dry and warm. He covered two of the crouching pheasants with his coat, rounding the back of it over them like a shell. The other boys did the same. They covered all the helpless pheasants. The small gray hens and the larger brown cocks. Now the boys felt the rain soaking through their shirts and freezing. They ran across the slippery fields, unsure of their footing, the ice clinging to their skin as they made their way toward the blurry lights of the house.

—Jim Heynen

Ten Ways of Looking at Pheasant Hunting in Southwestern Minnesota

1

kids about six
raced the neighborhood
long curling tail feathers
of the ringneck   trailing
from hands   head bands
magic

2

magic exploded up
from marsh grass
cornfields
wonderful thrumming
wings through nerves
that net of joy
        my being

3

swung the heavy
double gun
belched twice in bright
October sunlight   and sometimes feathers
burst from
became a halo
and the body of the ringneck stopped
dropped
thud into grass
feathers spinning
       lazily
         after
glinting happily
in the sun

4

bird in its jaws
the dog raced back through high grass
eyes filled
with the great light

5

wrung that rooster's neck
till headless it swirled
like a stepped-on snake
and spit   blood
onto khaki pants

6

the cold dead eye of the head
stared
at the hunter

7

days of striding
with the gun, the air
empty
the day's bag:
beggar's lice
cockleburs

8

at sunset
sitting on a tile
last cry
of the ringneck
over by the ditch

9

chemicals:
D-D-T, P-C-B, A-B-C-D-E-F-G . . .
black empty fields
no grass   flow
into sunset
winter habitat
bare and cold as steel
barrel of the gun
forgotten on the porch

—Joe Paddock

RIVERS OF THE COTEAU DES PRAIRIES

The broad, flat-iron-shaped Coteau des Prairies is an elevation of the plains of northeastern South Dakota, its northern tip just touching the North Dakota border and its eastern edge cutting the southwestern corner of Minnesota. This plateau, "the highland of the prairies" 500 to 800 feet higher than the central plains, is the most conspicuous surface feature in southwestern Minnesota and sets the topographic stage for the streams of the region.

The Coteau exists because it rests in part on a base of hard quartzitic rock, the remains of an ancient mountain range. Ridges of this very old rock resisted erosion for hundreds of millions of years, and glaciers deposited high moraines on top of the hard rock. Sioux quartzite, sometimes called red rock or jasper, crops out in several places in southwestern Minnesota, such as in the extreme southwest corner of the state, the "Blue Mound" along the Rock River, and in the quarry near the town of Pipestone. (Pipestone rock, or catlinite, from which Indians made their ceremonial pipes, is a softer layer of siltstone inter-bedded in the quartzite.)

The glacial moraines making up the plateau could even be termed rugged along the edge—early explorers looking back at the lowlands below must have had a feeling of being in high country. And although the top is generally smooth, the rolling topography is poorly drained and includes many lakes, ponds, and marshes, particularly within the northern tip in South Dakota where elevations are greater than in Minnesota.

All along the edge of the Coteau, small streams and creeks, some that flow only temporarily in normally dry ravines, run down the rugged slopes perpendicular to the plateau's edge. From the western edge in South Dakota, their waters eventually find their way to the Missouri; from Minnesota's eastern edge they flow into the Minnesota River Valley. Especially on the eastern side, small streams cut steep gorges and rugged valleys, where wooded, cool oases contrast sharply with surrounding wind-swept prairies. These gorges protected the woodlands from prairie fires and originally provided almost the only hardwood timber in this part of the plains.

Among the hills of the eastern edges of the Coteau in Minnesota are the headwaters of four of the state's major streams: the Lac qui Parle, Yellow Medicine, Redwood, and Cottonwood rivers, all flowing to the Minnesota Valley. Along the top of the plateau, but near the eastern edge, is the divide between the Minnesota-Mississippi drainage to the east and the Missouri drainage to the southwest. Here two other major rivers rise on top of the Coteau and flow south into Iowa, one from either side of the divide. The Des Moines River on the east eventually becomes Iowa's largest stream, emptying into the Mississippi after flowing southeast across the entire state of Iowa. And the Rock River, west of the divide, flows out of the most southwestern corner of Minnesota, soon into Iowa's Big Sioux River, and then to the Missouri.

Waters of the Coteau streams are generally hard, with alkalinities from about 150 to 200 p.p.m.; streams originating in the underground waters of the calcareous glacial drift are very hard. The highest alkalinities in this range occur in the waters of the deeply eroded Coteau slopes and of spring tributaries flowing on the Coteau and in the Minnesota Valley.

The four rivers emptying into the Minnesota—Lac qui Parle, Yellow Medicine, Redwood, and Cottonwood—share many characteristics. Each has three distinct reaches: a swift, rocky stretch as the headwaters come down the slope of the Coteau; a long, slow, meandering course across the lowland plains; and a deep rocky gorge section where waters plunge into the 200-foot-deep Minnesota River Valley. The headwaters are relatively clear, flowing through rapids and over gravel bars; the lowland stretches in the plains, where the channels are in glacial drift high in clay and extensively ditched, are turbid with suspended clay and flow over soft, silty bottoms; and in the lower gorge, although stream bottoms are generally of large rocks and boulders, the waters retain much silt from upstream reaches, and silt coats the rocks. In the low water of autumn and winter, however, the four rivers may become clear throughout their courses.

All four rivers begin on the Coteau at elevations of about 1,600 to 1,900 feet, drop sharply for the first 500 feet, level off at about 1,000 to 1,100 feet on the low plains, and empty into the Minnesota at about 800 to 900 feet. Gradients in the headwater reaches range to 50 feet per mile, 1 to 2 feet per mile on the lowlands, and up to 100 feet per mile in the Minnesota Valley gorge of the lower Redwood where many falls and cascades occur.

The lowland reaches of these four rivers may seem slow and uninteresting, especially because they have been extensively ditched and straightened, but some reaches resemble unmodified prairie streams, with winding bottomlands shaded by willows and cottonwoods. In these low plains sections some streams, such as the Cottonwood, follow courses set by glacial meltwaters that flowed southeast along the edge of the retreating ice.

In swift-water reaches, some stream sections have been set aside as state or local parks. In the upper reach of the Redwood, for example, is Camden State Park, a spacious section of densely wooded river valley, surprising but welcome amid the flat plains. Camden is much used for camping, picnicking, and hiking, and for skiing in winter; it is unique among the southwestern streams in having sufficient springwater tributaries to provide some trout habitat, and trophy browns are occasionally taken by trout fishermen. Lyon County's Garvin Park on the upper Cottonwood encloses a spreading, wooded valley of steep slopes and rushing stream, offering camping, picnicking, and trails.

The lower gorge reaches of all four rivers are outstanding areas of recreational use or historical significance. On the Lac qui Parle, northeast of the village of Dawson, is Lac qui Parle County Park, a large area with woods and open space for camping and other outdoor activities along the stream banks. The river here is rushing and noisy in high water, full of boulders and white water, flowing between high wooded banks. At the mouth of the Lac qui Parle in the Minnesota

River is Lac qui Parle State Park, and along the lake is the large Lac qui Parle Wildlife Management Area. Originally, the Lac qui Parle River formed a delta in the Minnesota Valley and impounded Lac qui Parle Lake, but the lake level is now controlled by a man-made dam. Near the lower end of the Yellow Medicine is the Upper Sioux Agency State Park, site of bloody Indian war

The park memorializes territorial supreme court jurist Charles Flandrau, a hero of the defense of New Ulm in the Sioux Uprising. It includes a swimming pool, camp and picnic grounds, primitive canoe access, and many trails.

The Rock River is unique in the state of Minnesota because it is the only one of Minnesota's major streams in the Missouri River drainage.

in the summer of 1862; this was also known as the Yellow Medicine Agency. Although the emphasis in this park is on the historical importance of the Indian agency, the Yellow Medicine River contributes its wild-water scenic beauty to the site. The gorge section of the Redwood River includes Alexander Ramsey City Park in Redwood Falls. The park contains some of the most unusual river environment in Minnesota. The swift rapids and cascades rushing over ancient granite are reminiscent of northern Minnesota, and the falls of Ramsey Creek, a straight, muddy ditch in its plains headwaters, plunges into the Minnesota Valley with beauty equal to the most remote waterfalls of the north. Many miles of trails, campgrounds, soaring bluffs of weathered granite, and rocky river rapids can be enjoyed in this island of wild river on the prairies. The lower Cottonwood flows through a wooded gorge and thence through Flandrau State Park at New Ulm.

The rest flow north to Hudson Bay, east through the Great Lakes and the St. Lawrence River to the Atlantic, or directly to the Mississippi as it courses through or along Minnesota.

Nevertheless, the Rock is not very different from other Minnesota streams originating on the Coteau des Prairies. The river's origins are in Pipestone County at an elevation of about 1,800 feet. From here it flows south, with much meandering, to the Iowa border. On farther, it empties into Iowa's Big Sioux River, which flows south through a central cleft on the Coteau to the Missouri.

The Rock River flows through a region that was undulating prairie, well drained by many small tributaries. There are no natural lakes in the watershed and little timber, although the main stream flows in a well-defined valley with occasional trees typical of riverbanks, such as cottonwood, willow, and soft maple. In the town of Luverne, a welcome shady city park is located by a bend of the river.

In addition to the Rock itself, several tributaries rise in Minnesota and join the Rock in Iowa—for example, Kanaranzi Creek and the Little Rock River (Nobles County). To the west, Flandreau, Pipestone, Beaver and Split Rock creeks originate in Pipestone and Rock counties and flow west into South Dakota, eventually emptying into the Big Sioux in Iowa. Split Rock Creek State Park offers camping, picnicking, a swimming beach on an artificial lake, and trails; the name is derived from some exposed red Sioux quartzite that was fractured and split by weathering. To the east, the headwaters of the Little Sioux rise in Jackson County, flow south into Iowa and toward the Missouri.

The main stem of the Rock flows over fifty miles in Minnesota, dropping about 450 feet from its headwaters in Pipestone County, an average gradient of about nine feet per mile; there are no precipitous rapids along its course. The Rock drains 558 square miles in Minnesota. Other tributaries of the Big Sioux River drain 921 square miles in Minnesota, then flow through either South Dakota or Iowa; to the east, the headwaters of the Little Sioux and tributaries drain 314 square miles of Minnesota land. The total Missouri River watershed in Minnesota is 1,793 square miles. The Rock River has a mean discharge near the Iowa border of about 100 cubic feet per second, although precise data are not available.

About two miles north of Luverne, overlooking the Rock River from the west, is a sharp escarpment of old, hard rock—Morton Gneiss, estimated to be 3.5 billion years old. Over this escarpment, the Sioux drove bison to their deaths—their way of harvesting part of the vast herds for meat, hide, and fur. This area is now set aside as Blue Mounds State Park, including camp and picnic grounds, an artificial lake (on Mound Creek, a small western tributary of the Rock), and trails. A herd of bison grazes this original prairie. The name of the park is derived from the appearance of the high mounds as viewed against the western sky by migrating settlers, but also perhaps from the bluish lichens that cover almost all exposed rock. This was the "The Rock" on Joseph N. Nicollet's map. It overlooks the meandering stream to which its name was given—Rock River.

—Thomas F. Waters

A STORY ABOUT MY FATHER

I'll tell you a story about my father. Each year men from south of us—Kansas, Missouri, Arkansas, even Alabama and Tennessee—would move through the country, following the small grain harvest north. They would end up in North Dakota or Canada about late September and would then go home again. My father, since he ran a threshing rig, would hire one or two of these men each threshing season. Sometimes I went with him, and at 6:00 a.m. before the rig had started, we would drive uptown to a small park in which some of the men had slept that night. If he saw a man with a face he liked, he would ask him if he could pitch bundles and drive a team of horses.

On one of those mornings, he hired a man whom I will call Garth Morrison, who had come up from a small town in Missouri. Garth turned out to be a good worker, and he and my father got on together very well.

He stayed with us during the week. On Saturday night, the teams put away, he would go to town, and be gone Saturday night and Sunday night. But early Monday morning he would always be back and ready for work.

One Monday morning he didn't show up. My father was puzzled, and at about 9:00 a.m. he put someone else in charge of the rig and drove to town to see if he could find Garth. Asking around here and there, he heard that Garth had been picked up by the sheriff Saturday night. Apparently he had made a date with a waitress at a cafe, who had agreed to let him walk her home. At 11:00 he had gone to pick her up and, probably to his surprise, she did let him walk her home, where she lived with her parents. A few words were exchanged—probably a series of misunderstood signals between a southern man and a northern woman. He slapped her face. She went inside furious and complaining. Her parents called the sheriff. The man was from out of state. The sheriff and the judge had a secret court session the next morning—Sunday morning—having refused all along to let Garth call my father on the telephone, and sentenced him to twenty years at Stillwater prison. By Sunday noon he was on his way to Stillwater. By Sunday night the sheriff was back in town. It was said he always tried to show proof of his vigilance shortly before an election.

My father, once he got the story from the reluctant sheriff, was enraged. He shut down the threshing rig, and with his best friend, Alvin Hofstad, got in the car and drove to St. Paul to see the attorney general of Minnesota. The attorney general agreed that the facts gave off a bad odor. He went with my father and Alvin Hofstad to Stillwater, where they talked to Garth and verified the story. He then had Garth taken out of the prison and returned to the county jail in Madison to await trial. He stayed in the county jail a month or more, and we as boys would go up to talk with him through the window. My father hired a lawyer and paid for Garth's wife and infant son to come up from Missouri for the trial. They stayed with us and she testified at the trial; I remember her holding the baby on the stand. The jury convicted Garth of simple assault, and the judge ruled that the time already spent in jail more than served out the appropriate sentence. He was released and the family returned to Missouri.

My father never spoke to the sheriff again for the rest of the sheriff's life. Garth did not come north again either. The spring following the trial, Garth and his wife invited my father and mother down to Missouri for a visit. They drove down, and it turned out that everyone in that small Missouri town knew the story. When my father went for a haircut, the barber would not let him pay, and whenever he and mother went into a restaurant, the owner would not accept their money.

To be able to respect your father is such a beautiful thing! I learned then that the indignation of the solitary man is the stone pin that connects this world to the next. The more easy-going businessmen in Madison, who had so many friends, would have left Garth sitting in his cell for twenty years. They would have been afraid to put their hand into the web of social relationships, afraid the web would not be repaired over night, or that the spider of loneliness would bite them. I learned too that when you have been unselfish, people respond not in words but by feeding you. I learned so much from that one story! We don't need to read books on ethics or to see documentaries on television; one moral example will do for a lifetime.

—Robert Bly

PRO PATRIA

I grew out of one war and into another. My father came from leaden ships of sea, from the Pacific theater; my mother was a WAVE. I was the offspring of the great campaign against the tyrants of the 1940's, one explosion in the Baby Boom, one of millions come to replace those who had just died. My bawling came with the first throaty note of a new army in spawning. I was bred with the haste and dispatch and careless muscle-flexing of a nation giving bridle to its own good fortune and success. I was fed by the spoils of 1945 victory.

I learned to read and write on the prairies of southern Minnesota.

Along the route used to settle South Dakota and the flatlands of Nebraska and northern Iowa, in the cold winters, I learned to use ice skates.

My teachers were brittle old ladies, classroom football coaches, flushed veterans of the war, pretty girls in sixth grade.

In patches of weed and clouds of imagination, I learned to play army games. Friends introduced me to the Army Surplus Store off main street. We bought dented relics of our fathers' history, rusted canteens and olive-scented, scarred helmet liners. Then we were our fathers, taking on the Japs and Krauts along the shores of Lake Okabena, on the flat fairways of the golf course. I rubbed my fingers across my father's war decorations, stole a tiny battle star off one of them and carried it in my pocket.

Baseball was for the summertime, when school ended. My father loved baseball. I was holding a Louisville Slugger when I was six. I played a desperate shortstop for the Rural Electric Association Little League team; my father coached us, and he is still coaching, still able to tick off the starting line-up of the great Brooklyn Dodger teams of the 1950's.

Sparklers and the forbidden cherry bomb were for the Fourth of July: a baseball game, a picnic, a day in the city park, listening to the high school band playing "Anchors Aweigh," a speech, watching a parade of American Legionnaires. At night, fireworks erupted over the lake, reflections.

It had been Indian land. Ninety miles from Sioux City, sixty miles from Sioux Falls, eighty miles from Cherokee, forty miles from Spirit Lake and the site of a celebrated massacre. To the north was Pipestone and the annual Hiawatha Pageant. To the west was Luverne and Indian burial mounds.

111

Norwegians and Swedes and Germans had taken the plains from the Sioux. The settlers must have seen endless plains and eased their bones and said, "Here as well as anywhere, it's all the same."

The town became a place for wage earners. It is a place for wage earners today—not very spirited people, not very thoughtful people.

Among these people I learned about the Second World War, hearing it from men in front of the courthouse, from those who had fought it. The talk was tough. Nothing to do with causes or reason; the war was right, they muttered and it had to be fought. The talk was about bellies filled with German lead, about the long hike from Normandy to Berlin, about close calls and about the origins of scars just visible on hairy arms. Growing up, I learned about another war, a peninsular war in Korea, a gray war fought by the town's Lutheran and Baptists. I learned about that war when the town hero came home, riding in a convertible, sitting straight-backed and quiet, an ex-POW.

The town called itself Turkey Capital of the World. In September the governor and some congressmen came to town. People shut down their businesses and came in from their farms. Together we watched trombones and crepe-paper floats move down main street. The bands and floats represented Sheldon, Tyler, Sibley, Jackson, and a dozen other neighboring towns.

Turkey Day climaxed when the farmers herded a billion strutting, stinking, beady-eyed birds down the center of town, past the old Gobbler Cafe, past Woolworth's and the Ben Franklin store and the Standard Oil service station. Feathers and droppings and popcorn mixed together in tribute to the town and the prairie. We were young. We stood on the curb and blasted the animals with ammunition from our pea-shooters.

We listened to Nelson Rockefeller and Karl Rölvaag and the commander of the Minnesota VFW, trying to make sense out of their words, then we went for twenty-five-cent rides on the Octopus and Tilt-A-Whirl.

I couldn't hit a baseball. Too small for football, but I stuck it out through junior high, hoping something would change. When nothing happened, I began to read. I read Plato and Erich Fromm, the Hardy Boys and enough Aristotle to make me prefer Plato. The town's library was quiet and not a very lively place—nothing like the football field on an October evening and not a very good substitute. I watched the athletes from the stands and cheered them at pep rallies, wishing I were with them. I went to homecoming dances, learned to drive an automobile, joined the debate team, took girls to drive-in theaters and afterwards to the A & W root beer stand.

I took up an interest in politics. One evening I put on a suit and drove down to the League of Women Voters meeting, embarrassing myself and some candidates and most of the women voters by asking questions that had no answers.

I tried going to Democratic party meetings. I'd read it was the liberal party. But it was futile. I could not make out the difference between the people there and the people down the street boosting Nixon and Cabot Lodge. The essential thing about the prairie, I learned, was that one part of it is like any other part.

At night I sometimes walked about the town. "God is both transcendent and imminent. That's Tillich's position." When I walked, I chose the darkest streets, away from the street lights. "But is there a God? I mean, is there a God like there's a tree or an apple? Is God a being?" I usually ended up walking toward the lake. "God is Being-Itself." The lake, Lake Okabena, reflected the town-itself, bouncing off a black-and-white pattern identical to the whole desolate prairie: flat, tepid, small, strangled by algae, shut in by middle-class houses, lassoed by a ring of doctors, lawyers, CPA's, dentists, drugstore owners, and proprietors of department stores. "Being-Itself? Then is this town God? It exists, doesn't it?" I walked past where the pretty girls lived, stopping long enough to look at their houses, all the lights off and the curtains drawn. "Jesus," I muttered, "I hope not. Maybe I'm an atheist."

One day in May the high school held graduation ceremonies. Then I went away to college, and the town did not miss me much.

—Tim O'Brien

Grateful acknowledgement is made to the following publishers and individuals for permission to reprint material in this book. Meridel Le Sueur's "The Ancient People and the Newly Come" from Chester Anderson, ed., *Growing Up in Minnesota*, University of Minnesota Press, 1976.   Joseph Amato's "The Countryside as Quilt" from *Countryside: A Mirror of Ourselves*, Crossings Press, 1981, reprinted with the author's permission.   Carol Bly's "Great Snows" from *Letters from the Country*, Harper and Row, 1981, reprinted with the author's permission.   Barton Sutter's "What the Countryman Knows by Heart," copyright © 1993 by Barton Sutter, reprinted from *The Book of Names*, with the permission of BOA Editions, Ltd., 260 East Ave., Rochester, NY 14604. Nancy Paddock's "Going Out to Get the Mail," reprinted with the author's permission. "On the Coteau des Prairies, 1838" from *Joseph N. Nicollet on the Plains and Prairies: The Expeditions of 1838-39 With Journals, Letters and Notes on the Dakota Indians*, translated and edited by Edmund C. Bray and Martha Coleman Bray, pages 67-71 (St. Paul: Minnesota Historical Society Press, 1976; repr. ed. 1993). Bill Holm's "Horizontal Grandeur" from *The Music of Failure*, Plains Press, 1986, reprinted with the author's permission. Phil Dacey's "Picking Rock" from *The Man in the Red Suspenders*, Milkweed Editions, 1986, reprinted with the author's permission. Paul Gruchow's "Bones" from *Grass Roots: The Universe of Home*, Milkweed Editions 1995, reprinted with the author's permission. "Henry Thoreau in Redwood Falls" from Franklin B. Sanborn, *The Familiar Letters of Henry David Thoreau*, Houghton Mifflin, 1894. "Toward the Sunset" from *Giants in the Earth* by O. E. Rolvaag, copyright 1927 by Harper & Row, Publishers, Inc., renewed 1955 by Jeannie Marie Berdahl Rolvaag, reprinted by permission of HarperCollins Publishers, Inc. Baron E. de Mandat-Gracey's "Pullman Cars and Their Occupants" from William Conn, translator and editor, *Cow-boys and Colonels: Narrative of a Journey Across the Prairie and over the Black Hills of Dakota*, London: Griffith, Farran, Okeden & Welsh, 1887. Phebe Hansen's "Cottonwoods" from *Sacred Hearts*, Milkweed Editions, 1985, reprinted with the author's permission. "Bill Holm's "In an Icelandic Graveyard" from Tom Guttormsson, Bill Holm, and John Resmerski, eds., *Happy Birthday, Minneota*, Westerheim Press, 1981, used with the author's permission. David Pichaske's "The Grandfathers" from *Visiting the Father and Other Poems*, Dacotah Territory, 1987. Hamlin Garland's "The Land of the Straddle-Bug" from *A Son of the Middle Border*, Macmillan, 1917. "Reflections in Sleepy Eye" from Collected Poems 1947-1980 by Allen Ginsberg, copyright 1984 by Allen Ginsberg, reprinted by permission of HarperCollins Publishers, Inc. "Home," from *Lake Wobegon Days,* by Garrison Keillor; copyright © 1985 by Garrison Keillor; used by permission of Viking Penguin, a division of Penguin Putnam, Inc. Leo Dangel's "How to Take a Walk" from *Home from the Field*, Spoon River Poetry Press, 1997, reprinted with the author's permission. Frederick Manfred's "My Father" from *Prime Fathers*, Salt Lake City: Howe Brothers, 1988, used with the permission of Freya Manfred. Faith Sullivan's "Learning to Swim" from *The Cape Ann*, Crown Publishers, 1988, reprinted with the author's permission.   Jim Heynen's "What Happened During the Ice Storm" from *The One-Room Schoolhouse*, Knopf, 1993, reprinted with the author's permission. Joe Paddock's "Ten Ways of Looking at Pheasant Hunting in Southwestern Minnesota" from Tom Guttormsson, Bill Holm, and John Resmerski, eds., *Happy Birthday, Minneota*, Westerheim Press, 1981, reprinted with the author's permission. Thomas F. Waters' "The Rocks and Rivers of the Coteau des Prairies" from *The Streams and Rivers of Minnesota*, University of Minnesota Press, 1977. Robert Bly, "A Story About My Father" from "Being a Lutheran Boy-God in Minnesota" in Chester Anderson, ed., *Growing Up in Minnesota*, University of Minnesota Press, 1976, reprinted with the author's permission. Tom Hennen's "Autumn Waiting" from *Looking Into the Weather*, Westerheim Press, 1983, reprinted with the author's permission. Tim O'Brien's "Pro Patria" from *If I Die in a Combat Zone*, Delacorte Press/Seymour Lawrence, 1973, reprinted with the author's permission.